LOUISIANA'S GERMAN HERITAGE

Louis Voss' Introductory History

Edited by Don Heinrich Tolzmann

HERITAGE BOOKS
2012

HERITAGE BOOKS
AN IMPRINT OF HERITAGE BOOKS, INC.

Books, CDs, and more—Worldwide

For our listing of thousands of titles see our website
at
www.HeritageBooks.com

A Facsimile Reprint
Published 2012 by
HERITAGE BOOKS, INC.
Publishing Division
100 Railroad Ave. #104
Westminster, Maryland 21157

Cover illustration is a sculpture of the Louisiana Purchase
made by Karl Bitter in 1803. The photograph of the
sculpture is from Rudolph Cronau's, *Drei Jahrhunderte
Deutchen Lebens in Amerika*, published in 1909

International Standard Book Numbers
Paperbound: 978-1-55613-979-6
Clothbound: 978-0-7884-9372-0

iii

Table of Contents

Editor's Preface   vii

Editor's Introduction   ix

Officers and Directors of the German Society   2

Foreword   4

The German Element in the National Life of America   6

The Germans in Louisiana History   48

History of the German Society   74

Conclusion   92

Addendum   95

Appendix   97

Notes   113

Sources for Further Reading   118

LIST OF PHOTOGRAPHS APPEARING IN THIS BOOK

	Page
Blaffer, G. Ad.	49
Blaise, Peter	31
Buck, Chas. F.	15
Bultmann, A. F.	55
Deiler, J. H.	3
Del Bondio, E. F.	51
Frantz, H. L.	45
Frantz, Wm.	7
Frotscher, Richard	47
Gabert, Dr. H. A.	5
Gross, Josiah	59
Haller, P.	63
Hassinger, J.	49
Hecht, Rudolph	27
Heintz, Rev. L. P.	35
Holzer, R. J.	41
Jahncke, F.	37
Jung, P.	67
Jurgens, George	53
Knoop, O.	39
Koch, Julius	47
Kolb, C.	21
Koelle, Rev. F. O.	33
Krause, R.	23
Mayer, Phil. D.	43
Merz, Val.	61
Odenheimer, S.	19
Prager, B.	11
Reuther, Jos.	9
Rickert, F.	69
Ricks, A. G.	17
Rueff, George W.	71
Schoen, J.	45
Vonderbank, M.	57
Voss, Rev. Louis	13
Walsdorf, E. H.	65
Weiblen, A.	25
Wirth, Chas.	29

Editor's Preface

In the 19th century, New Orleans became one of the major German-American urban centers in the South. However, this and other aspects of Louisiana German history are not generally well known. The purpose of this work is to make this new edition of Louis Voss' introductory history again available, so that this rich heritage would be illuminated. Originally published in 1927 for the 80th anniversary of the German Society of New Orleans, this work provides a general introduction to the topic together with a history of the German Society, as well as a survey of German-American history at the national level. (1) The increased interest in German-American Studies in general and in Louisiana's German heritage in particular necessitated this new edition. (2)

DHT

Editor's Introduction

According to the 1990 U.S. Census, the German element of Louisiana constitutes 12% of the state's total population of 4.2 millions. (1) Louisiana is, however, generally associated with its French heritage, which is not surprizing as those of French descent account for 23.3% of the state's population. Moreover, Louisiana stood under French dominion from 1682, when LaSalle claimed it for France, until 1763, when it became a Spanish colony until 1801 when it was returned to France, which kept it until 1803 when Napoleon sold the vast territory known as the Louisiana Purchase to the U.S.

As John Frederick Nau has observed "the Germans' part in building an important city in the lower Mississippi valley has to a great extent been overshadowed by the predominant work of the French and the Spanish." Indeed, in the 1950s, Nau observed that considerable surprize is often registered "when one ventures to suggest that other Europeans besides the French and Spanish have had a part in the forging of New Orleans life, among these the immigrants from Germany." (2)

A second reason for the lack of general awareness of Louisiana's German heritage can be found in the two world wars, which obscured the German dimension in American history. Nau noted that this was a problem not unique to the history of Louisiana, but was a problem pertaining to American history in general. He wrote that "if one looks over the works treating the origin, history, and accomplishments of the American nation, to ascertain what part the descendants of the millions of German immigrants took in the development of the country, " one rarely finds more than a brief mention. (3)

Reinhard Kondert observes that "despite the recognized significance of the German element among Louisiana's colonial officials, historians of Louisiana have displayed an amazing ignorance of that fact." He also notes that only in the recent past "have scholars come to admit that the Germans played a crucial role in the development" of the state. (4) This recent awareness of the role of the German heritage in American history is, of course, due to the ethnic heritage/roots revival of the 1960s/70s. Since that time, German-American Studies as an academic field of study have flourished. This has caused a re-examination of how American history has been written at the national, state, regional, and local levels.

The German element constitutes not only the largest ethnic element in 20 states of the Union, but is also the nation's largest ethnic group in the entire country. Outside of the 20 states where German-Americans are the largest group, there are a number of areas where the German heritage is especially strong, e.g. in Texas, California, and Florida. However, the one state which has usually been overlooked has been Lousiana. Recent works dealing with Lousiana's German heritage have contributed greatly to rectifying this oversight, and have also re-established continuity with the valuable German-American historical publications completed before the First World War.

Louisiana has a long history with regard to its German heritage, which reaches back to the early 1700s. Indeed, the first Germans arrived there in 1718. The German immigration became so concentrated that the area near New Orleans became known already in the 18th century as the "German Coast." And the Germans settlers there acquired a reputation as well. In 1803, the colonial prefect of Louisiana and commissioner of the French government, wrote to the French minister of the interior that the German Coast was "the most industrious, the most populous, the most at ease, the most upright, the most respected part" of the French colony. Moreover, he advised that 1,000-1,200 German settlers per year should be encourgaged to come to Louisiana. (5)

New Orleans became especially important for the German immigration as it was one of the four major ports of entry for recently arrived German immigrants, along with New York, Philadelphia, and Baltimore. Although most immigrants moved north into the Mississippi River Valley, or east into the Ohio River Valley, some remained in Louisiana, especially in New Orleans.

The first German book dealing with Louisiana was a German translation of Louis Hennepin's work, which was entitled *Der Landschafft Louisiana...*, (Nürnberg: Andrea Otto, 1689). Thereafter, the German facination and interest would continue, as is reflected in the various books published in the German states, which dealt with the new colony. (6)

By the beginning of the 19th century, the early German settlements in Louisiana were not only well known in Germany, but were providing the basis for literary works. In 1804, Heinrich Zschokke published his novel, *Die Prinzessin von Wolfenbüttel*, which is based on the legend of a German princess who emigrated with her friends to America to escape from the cruel treatment of her husband. The novel accompanies the princess to Louisiana, where her group establishes a German colony, Christinental. The novel describes the journey to America, the Mississippi River, the city of New Orleans, and the life of planters in Louisiana, and the wars amongst the Indian tribes. The novel was written with "a romantic splendor," as well as a sense of realism. The publication of such a work, obviously, added increased interest in Germany for Louisiana. (7)

In 1822-24, Paul Wilhelm, Duke of Württemberg, traveled widely through America, and visited New Orleans during his sojourn. He described New Orleans as "a gathering place of many nations," which had "a cosmopolitan population similar to that of the large transatlantic seaports." He also describes his visits there with prominent German-Americans, such as Vincent Nolte, and alludes to the presence of German-American churches and institutions. When Charles Sealsfield (Karl Postl), the famous German-American author visited Louisiana in 1827, he noted that "there are a great number of Germans in New Orleans." He notes that the newcomers are "either planters, farmers, merchants, or mechanics," and then proceeds to describe conditions in the state, which would be useful to prospective immigrants. Several other works, published in the first half of the 19th century also dealt with Louisiana, and no doubt contributed to interest in the area. (8)

In 1854-55, Ludwig von Reizenstein published his notorious novel, *Die Geheimnisse von New Orleans*, which no doubt added interest in the topic of Louisiana and its German element. (9) It should also be noted that by the mid-19th century Louisiana had also figured in several other works by German-American authors. For example, Gustav Brühl published *Charlotte. Eine Episode aus der Colonial-Geschichte Louisianas* (Cincinnati: Mecklenborg & Rosenthal, 1883), a literary work set in colonial Louisiana. It also would become the central focus of works published in the early 1900s, which aimed to describe Louisiana as a destination for German immigrations. The impact such works had on German-Americans and on Germans in Europe was that attention was focused on Louisiana, and this no doubt contributed to the German image of the state, and thereby to the German immigration and settlement. (10)

Indeed, New Orleans developed a flourishing German-American community by the mid-19th century. After 1840, German immigration increased substantially. In 1847, the German Society of New Orleans was founded to assist with the recently arrived immigrants. From 1850 to 1855, more than 125,000 Germans arrived at the port of New Orleans. In 1860, there were 24,614 German-born residents of Louisiana, most of whom resided in and around New

Orleans. By 1870, New Orleans alone had a German-speaking population of 25,000, or one-fifth of the city's population. There were not only German-American religious congregations, but numerous German-American societies as well. In the history of the state, more than 50 German-language newspapers and journals have been published. When the Civil War broke out, the Lousiana Germans placed 11 military companies into the field. Clearly, New Orleans was a major German-American center in the South. (11)

The presence of many fine German singing societies led to the sponsorship in New Orleans in 1890 of the national Sängerfest of the North American Sängerbund. This drew national, as well as international attention, to New Orleans as a German-American cultural center. By the turn of the century, German immigrants were actively recruited by the state by means of German-language brochures advertising the state as a place to settle. By the early 1900s, there were 32 German-American societies in the state, mainly in New Orleans. In 1909, a state branch of the German-American National Alliance was formed, which united the German-American societies of the state under one central organization. German instruction was available not only in the public schools, but was also available in the private and parochial schools maintained by German-American religious and secular organizations and institutions.

As one of the state's largest ethnic groups, the Louisiana Germans obviously became a target of the anti-German hysteria of World War One. Although they were only ca. 12% of the state's population, they had a history dating back to the eary 1700s, and were geographically concentrated historically in New Orleans and in the area near the city known as the German Coast. Moreover, they had an extensive network of religous and secular institutions and organizations, as well as a high quality German-American press. Also because New Orleans had been one of the major port cities of the German immigration, many German-Americans in the West and Midwest had come through the city, and continued to maintain ties with the city.

These cultural assocations were strengthened historically by the Missisippi River, which connected New Orleans with cities, towns, and settlements throughout the river valleys of the Missippi and Ohio Rivers. All of these factors, together with the 1890 Sängerfest and the German-American Alliance of Louisiana, contributed to making New Orleans a recognized German-American cultural center before the First World War. Another important factor was that the Louisiana Germans were especially fortunate to have in New Orleans not only one of the major German-American historians of the pre-World War One era, but also one of the foremost spokesmen of the German element in America: Prof. J. Hanno Deiler (1849-1909).

In 1879, Deiler accepted a position as Professor of German at Tulane University, a position he held for 27 years. It was Deiler who not only organized the 1890 Sängerfest in New Orleans, but also played an active role in the German-American community of the state. In 1895, he became President of the German Society of New Orleans, and in 1899, at the national convention of the North American Sängerbund in Cincinnati, Deiler was elected National President, an indication of his national reputation. He was without question one of the most "distinguished figures in the cultural life" of his time, and was well known for "his unbounded energy, his genial attitude toward students, and his untiring enthusiasm." (12) Following hard on the heels of the period of Deiler's life, was the tragedy of World War I.

An example of the severity of the anti-German hysteria of World War One in Louisiana is reflected in a law passed on 5 July 1918 by the Louisiana State Legislature. Act No. 114 was "An Act to prohibit the teaching of the German language in the public and private elementary and high schools, colleges, universities and other educational institutions in the State of Louisisana; and to provide penalties for the violation of this Act." (13)

This anti-German Act made it unlawful for "any teacher, professor, lecturer, person, or persons" in Louisiana "to teach the German language to any pupil or class." The Act further stipulated that any person violating the Act would be fined from $25.00 to $100.00, or be imprisoned from 10 to 90 days, or both, at the discretion of the judge. Moreover, each and every day that a person would violate the Act, would be regarded as a separate offense, "and punishable under the foregoing provisions." This hateful Act, obviously, struck a blow to the German heritage, as it eliminated German instruction not only in public educational institutions, but in the private and parochial schools maintained by the German-Americans of Lousiana. Fortunately, the Act was repealed by the State Legislature in 1921. (14)

Nationally, the 1920s were a time for recovery and reconstruction after the devasting years of the anti-German hysteria of World War One. An important occasion took place in 1927 with the celebration of the 80th anniversary of the German Society of New Orleans. And in 1928, the Deutsches Haus was founded in New Orleans to bring together the German-American societies of the city under one umbrella organization.

In 1935, Karl J. R. Arndt accepted a position as Professor of German at Louisiana State University. During his time in Louisiana (he remained with LSU until 1947), Arndt began his research on the German-American press with May E. Olson of the Louisiana State University Library. This resulted in the publication in 1961 of a major work in the field of German-American Studies, which listed state by state, and city by city, all the German-American newspapers and journals, which had been published from 1732 to 1955. (15)

Arndt became, not surprizingly, interested in Louisiana's facinating German heritage, and investigated and researched several German communities in the state. He was especially interested in the settlement, Germantown, "a forgotten German colony in Northwestern Louisiana near the town of Minden." (16) He became especially interested in this communitarian settlement as it related to other similar German settlements in Pennsylvania and Ohio. (17)

In 1941, when Arndt edited a collection of German-American stories for use in German instruction, he included one by Friedrich Gerstäcker entitled "Sieben Tage auf einem amerikanischen Dampfboot," which dealt with experiences during a week's journey on a Mississippi River steamboat, which operated out of New Orleans. (18)

In the 1950s, when Nau wrote his history of the German element in New Orleans, he observed that "the determination and loyalty of the German people, which had motivated them to build so well in the former century, continued to inspire them." He found this to be apparent "in the continuation of their churches, schools, and singing and benevolent societies, as well as in their businesses and industries, many of which continue operation to this very day." (19)

Nau also observed that "in the land of crawfish bisque and creole shrimp and gumbo," it was possible to find "the German Gemütlichkeit, to dine on German foods at Kolb's restaurant and to drink beer made by a German-trained brewmaster, to attend a church and a school founded by German people in the last century, and to enjoy German songs by visiting the Deutsches Haus on a Thursday evening, where husky yet loyal voices give their all in singing Lieder." He noted that "the influence of the German upon the city of New Orleans still lives," while German-American contributions to the building of New Orleans "are visible on every hand." (20)

As elsewhere nationally, the German heritage was again on the upswing by the late 1950s, and in 1958 the National Sängerfest of the North American Sängerbund was held in New Orleans. A recent directory of German-American societies listed a variety of societies and organizations in Louisiana, an indication of continued, but growing interest in the German heritage. (21)

Recently, Ellen C. Merrill, Professor of German at Dillard University, has played an important role in German heritage activities in the state. Among her major accomplishments has been leading the establishment of the German Interpretive Center (museum) in New Orleans. She was also instrumental in the re-establishment of an annual German Day in New Orleans, complete with parades and social activities for the community. She was also instrumental in the creation of the German-Americana archives at the Historic New Orleans Collection. (22)

Although the German element of Louisiana is not the largest one in the state, there can be no doubt that it is an important one because of its substantial contributions in the history of Louisiana. Nau commented that in the research for his history of the New Orleans Germans, he repeatedly heard remarks that German-Americans were the people "who helped to make New Orleans a city of commerce, industry, and business. They built New Orleans." He concluded that "To read the history of New Orleans and Louisiana aright, it is important to consider carefully the part played by the German element of the city in molding the culture and life of this American city." An old Creole expression in New Orelans states "It takes German people to do that!" (23)

The author of this volume, Louis Voss, served as Pastor of the First German Presbyterian Church of New Orleans (see his biography, p. 13). This work, obviously, aimed to accomplish a threefold purpose. First, it was completed for the 80th anniversary of the German Society of New Orleans, so it traced the history of the Society. Second, it provides a survey of the German dimension in the history of the state of Louisiana. Third, it begins with, and places the history of the Louisiana Germans and the German Society within the broader context of national German-American history.

It should be noted that this work was published only nine years after the anti-German hysteria of World War One, and that this work, hence, aimed to re-assert and re-emphasize the role German-Americans had played nationally, as well as in the state of Louisiana. By emphasizing the 80th anniversary of the German Society, it demonstrated that the German element had weathered the storm and stress of the war years.

Moreover, the works stresses three points (pp. 44ff) in response to the question as to what lessons can be learned from American history. First, it stresses that America "is not an Anglo-Saxon nation, but a composite people." Here it should be noted that, German-Americans in the 1920s were already articulating and pioneering a multicultural outlook, which was a half century ahead of its time. Second, the work notes that "truth and pride should induce descendants of Germans to keep alive the memory of their forebears in America." This was felt to be especially important in the light of the anti-German propaganda of the recent world war. This had resulted in the "inadequate" treatment of the role German-Americans had played in American history. This was something which should be rectified, so that the German dimension could be appreciated. Lastly, the work notes that a lesson to be learned from history is that German-Americans should "perpetuate the virtues" of their ancestors, and cultivate the German language. They have "a right and a duty" to do so, as do the other ethnic groups in the U.S., according to Voss. Certainly, it could be said that Voss and other German-American historians were pioneer forerunners of cultural pluralism, an outlook which by the latter decades of the 20th century had become widely accepted as a realistic desription of the realities of American life.

To this new edition the editor has added a new preface, introduction, notes, an appendix dealing with J. Hanno Deiler, and references to sources for further reading. (24)

OFFICERS AND DIRECTORS

JOSEPH REUTHER ....President
BRUNO PRAGER ....First Vice-President
FRANK LANGBEHN ....Second Vice-President
DR. J. M. KOELLE ....Treasurer
PAUL SCHWARTZ ....Recording Secretary
JOSEPH ENGEL ....Financial Secretary

JOSEPH REUTHER	CHAS. W. EICHLING	ALBERT WEIBLEN
BRUNO PRAGER	PAUL J. SENDKER	M. S. SENTON
PAUL SCHWARTZ	FRANK MOLITOR	THEO. BRUNE
DR. J. M. KOELLE	HENRY ORTLAND	FRANK LANGBEHN
OTTO ABELE	HENRY KRAAK	ARNO BEIER
PROF. DR. HERM.. GESSNER		M. G. RAPP

INVESTIGATING COMMITTEE.
WILLIAM FRANTZ, Chairman.   J. D. JUNIUS,   THEO. BRUNE.

FINANCE COMMITTEE.
M. S. SENTON. Chairman. BRUNO PRAGER, FRANK LANGBEHN

AGENCY COMMITTEE.
FRANK MOLITOR, Chairman.   OTTO ABELE,   HENRY KRAAK.

ARCHIVES COMMITTEE.
P. J. SENDKER, Chairm. Prof.Dr.HERM. B. GESSNER, JOS. ENGEL

LIST OF MEMBERS AND YEAR OF ADMITTANCE

OTTO ABELE 1920	FRANK MOLITOR 1915
A. C. AHRENS 1916	GEO. MUELLER 1927
ERNST ALBRECHT 1915	SIGMUND ODENHEIMER ..1916
A. BAEHRING 1925	HENRY ORTLAND 1915
ARNO BEIER 1924	JOSEPH PISTORIUS 1912
DAVID BONHAGE 1917	BRUNO PRAGER 1915
ERNST BORNEMANN 1910	Rt. Rev. J. F. PRIM 1927
WILLIAM BRUENE 1915	M. G. RAPP 1924
THEODORE BRUNE 1910	GEO. REDERSHEIMER 1915
C. W. EICHLING 1915	JOSEPH REUTHER 1902
A. EHNI 1925	STANLEY RAY 1924
LUDWIG EISEMANN 1915	PHILIP G. RICKS 1927
JOSEPH ENGEL 1923	GEO. SCHANZBACH 1906
JOHN W. ENGELHARDT 1924	RUDOLPH SCHULZE 1927
WILLIAM FRANTZ 1877	PAUL SCHWARTZ 1912
LOUIS C. FRANTZ 1925	THEODORE SCHLITZ 1927
Prof.Dr.HERM.B.GESSNER, 1916	PAUL J. SENDKER 1898
OTTO GOTTSCHO 1927	M. S. SENTON ....
JOSIAH GROSZ 1926	Dr. EDUARD SETHE 1926
Dr. JOHN GEO. HARZ 1920	GEO. SPRINGER 1923
Rev. Dr. MAX HELLER 1916	A. G. SIBBERS 1925
A. HERMANN 1927	LUDWIG STEIN 1927
D. J. JUNIUS 1924	EDWARD TIEMANN 1927
KONRAD KOLB 1902	WILLIAM TWICKLER 1924
FERDINAND KOELLE 1912	PHILIP VEITH 1921
Dr. J. MARCUS KOELLE 1912	HENRY VEITH 1923
HENRY KRAAK 1924	ALBERT WEIBLEN 1894
FRANK LANGBEHN 1898	G. WELLBAT 1927
Dr. OTTO LERCH 1916	CHAS. WERMUTH 1926
JULIUS C. H. MAYER........1927	HENRY WEIL ....

JOHN HANNO DEILER

John Hanno Deiler, educator and historian, was born at Altoetting, Bavaria, August 8, 1849. In 1868 he graduated from the Royal Normal College of Munich with high honors. He held government appointments in several schools as a teacher. In 1871 he became principal of a German school in New Orleans. In 1879 he was appointed professor of German at the University of Louisiana (now Tulane University). He was for many years a director and president of the "German Society"; originator of the German archives for the history of the Germans in the South. He founded the famous New Orleans Quartette Club in 1882. He was director general and leader of the great mass-chorus of the North American Singers' Union Saengerfest, held in New Orleans in February, 1890.

His historical researches relate chiefly to the Germans in the United States. He published "Germany's Contribution to the Present Population of New Orleans"; "The System of Redemption in the State of Louisiana"; "History of the German Churches of All Denominations in the State of Louisiana"; "Louisiana, a Home for German Settlers"; and "History of the German Society of New Orleans".

Professor Deiler was married December 9, 1872, to Wilhelmina, daughter of Paul Saganowsky, a well-known engineer.

FOREWORD

Thirty years ago, on the occasion of the Golden Jubilee of the German Society of New Orleans, J. Hanno Deiler, then professor of German language and literature at Tulane University, published a book in German, in which he reviewed the history of the German Society and its activities during a half century.

As the Eightieth Anniversary of this Society approaches, it was thought appropriate and wise to issue a pamphlet in English, so that all our fellow-citizens might be informed of the work the Society has carried on for so many years, with the hope that the sympathetic interest of the general public and a more active participation in its work, especially by those of German descent, might be aroused. With this aim in view, the following pages are submitted.

We also append some historic sketches, by the Editor and others, describing the share which Germans have had in the colonization and development of our country and especially of our own State of Louisiana, which will convince the impartial reader that Americans of German descent have every reason to be proud of their origin and will not fail to stimulate them to be equally loyal to this country, whether it be their adopted or their native land, in which so many Germans have rendered heroic service and many others, by their thrift and industry, have so largely contributed to the prosperity of the nation.

DR. HUGO ARTHUR GABERT

This prominent physician was born in Ryczywol, now Ritschenwalde, May 5, 1852. After he had successfully attended the high school in Rogassen, he decided to emigrate to the United States. In 1869 he landed in New York on his way to Chicago, where he remained until 1873. Then he came to New Orleans, where he studied medicine and became a physician whose skill and scrupulousness earned him the highest esteem of his fellowmen.

Dr. Gabert was a diligent member of the following societies: Druids, Knights of Pythias, Young Men's Gymnastic Club, Orleans Parish Medical Society, and the German Society of New Orleans. Especially the German Society is greatly indebted to Dr. Gabert for his numerous activities in the field of philanthropy.

Dr. Gabert was married to Miss Augusta Brandner in 1883. This union was blessed with five children: Mrs. James L. Bonnot, Mrs. George J. Peterson, Mrs. L. T. Donaldson, Mrs. Albert L. Forschler and August G. Gabert.

Dr. Gabert died at his summer home in Mandeville, La., January 10, 1923, lamented by all who knew him.

THE GERMAN ELEMENT IN THE NATIONAL LIFE OF AMERICA

For reasons of historical truth, as well as from justifiable pride of ancestry, Americans of German descent, near and remote, should be better informed and stress more emphatically the large number and the great achievements of their forefathers on American soil. This should be done not in a spirit of conceit, or to belittle the contributions of other racial elements to the greatness of this cosmopolitan nation, but simply to uphold the truth of history, to do justice to our German-American forefathers and to strengthen in their descendants the love of "the rock from which they were hewn."

DR. PHIL. VOLLMER.

The following article, written by the Editor of this pamphlet, appeared in The Daily Picayune on Sunday, October 12, 1913. It was illustrated by pictures of Baron von Steuben, Johann De Kalb, H. Steinway, John A. Roebling, Eberhard Faber and Thos. Nast.

Ever since America was colonized, immigration has been a matter of vital importance to this country. But for the constant stream of immigrants to its shores, our country would not be what it is today. The newcomers and their descendants have made the United States the great and rich nation we are.

It has always been the proud claim of America that it is the asylum of the oppressed the world over. All countries of Europe have furnished their quota of humanity seeking in this country a haven of rest from political, religious and social oppression and a field of activity to improve their material condition. No single European country can justly claim to be the mother country of the American republic. Though the original thirteen colonies owed allegiance to Great Britain, it is doubtful if there would be any United States today were it not for the part taken in the revolution by the German settlers. It is more likely we should have an English dominion like Canada.

It is customary in some quarters to claim an English origin for whatever lasting good has been done in this country and to refer to our American civilization as "Anglo-Saxon," utterly ignoring the large share the Germans, Scandinavians, Dutch, Swiss as well as the French have had in building and forming the American nation. Official figures give the number of Germans emigrating to the United States during the period from 1821 to 1900 from the German Empire and Switzerland as 6,895,478. The figures would be much larger if Germans from Alsace-Lorraine prior to 1870 had not been entered as Frenchmen, and Germans from Russian colonies as Russians. The immigration from Great

WILLIAM FRANTZ

For fifty years a member of the German Society, an honorary director and its honorary president.

For a biographical sketch of his life, see page 91.

Britain during the same period was only 3,024,222, and that from Ireland 3,871,253. Taking into consideration the vast immigration from other countries, it is seen that the Anglo-Saxon influx has formed but a very small fraction of the total.

The Germans and the Revolutionary War

As early as 1772 influential Germans of Philadelphia organized a society to encourage resistance to British authority in the colonies. After the Boston tea party episode they appointed a committee to correspond with their German kinsmen of the other colonies urging them to get ready for the conflict which, to their minds, was inevitable, by putting the militia in shape and forming new military organizations, while those who could not enlist for any reason were to be urged to contribute to the patriotic cause according to their ability.

When the great revolutionary storm broke out, the German colonists sided almost unanimously with the cause of freedom. From all German settlements, from Georgia to the Mohawk Valley, the volunteers streamed to Washington's banners, and while they helped to win the decisive battles, those that remained at home guarded the frontiers of the West against hostile incursions from the English and the Indians. It has often been told and sung how young Pastor Mühlenberg, the later general and friend of Washington, at the close of his farewell sermon to his German congregation in Virginia, slipped off his cape and stood in full armor in the pulpit, while the congregation jubilantly sang "Ein' Feste Burg Ist Unser Gott" (A Mighty Fortress Is Our God). No less renowned is the deed of Herkeimer, who, at the head of 8,000 men, nearly all Germans, threw himself against twice as many Englishmen and Indians and inflicted upon them a defeat which proved decisive for the surrender of Burgoyne at Saratoga, and, indeed, for the whole war. Two other Germans made names for themselves as generals in the War of the Revolution, De Kalb and Von Steuben.

The Germans as Farmers

The great West was not won for civilization by the Anglo-Saxons. This honor belongs pre-eminently to the German farmers who formed the vanguard of that invasion so far-reaching in its results. In course of time they were joined by the Anglo-Celts, the so-called Scotch-Irish, and the two races frequently intermingled, but the Germans were pathfinders and turned the forest and the prairie into luxuriant fields of grain.

Of all the nations gathered in this country, the Germans—in Colonial as well as modern times—have been acknowledged to be the most successful cultivators of the soil. Other pioneers usually started by cutting the bark of the trees and waited till they had rotted and therefore were unable for some years to raise any crops, while the Germans began at once to make a real clearing by felling and uprooting the trees and burning so much of the wood as was not needed for building and fencing purposes. Year by year this clearing was enlarged and soon the German settler had a fine farm, while those of other nationalities

JOSEPH REUTHER

Born in Deidesheim, Rheinpfalz. Arrived in New Orleans in 1886. Started in the baking business in 1892. Built up the best and most up-to-date bakery plant in the city. Elected to Orleans Parish School Board in 1908. His first and most important work on that board was the introduction of the teaching of the German language in the New Orleans High Schools the same year. Reappointed by Governor Pleasant in 1915 and re-elected for another term in 1916. Served for a number of years as a member of the Board of Directors of the Metropolitan Bank; helped to organize the Orleans Homestead Association, and served as first president for six years.

Member of the German Society since 1894 and president for the last six years.

were still relying on the chase for sustenance, or trading skins from the Indians for whisky. The Germans also understood the value of meadow land for pasture and chose their land accordingly. While others allowed their horses and cattle to stay in the fields during the winter, the Germans put them into stables and fed them well. They built large barns to house their crops, even before they thought of building a comfortable home for themselves. They introduced the culture of wheat, of fruits and flowers and of grapes, and in more recent years were the first to reclaim wet lands by drainage. Today, as 200 years ago, German farms are easily recognized by the magnitude of their barns, the neatness of their houses, the cleanliness of their yards, and to this day the Germans are the chief producers of vegetables and flowers in this country. It is evident that the German immigration has added immensely to the wealth of the country.

The Germans in Other Professions

Germans in other professions, besides that of the farmer, have taken a leading part in the development of this country. German artisans have always been in demand on account of their thorough training in their trades. German skilled workmen, chemists and civil engineers have contributed largely in developing the large modern industries. Andrew Carnegie has said that he owes a part of his great success to the German chemists whom he wisely engaged to analyze the ores that went into his furnaces.

The German engineer, Roebling, built the first Brooklyn bridge, the eighth wonder of the world, and the first bridge over Niagara.

The first book ever printed in this country was a German Bible. It was published in 1742. Not until forty years later did the first English Bible printed on American soil appear. The printer of this German Bible, Christoph Saur, also published a German almanac in 1738, which appeared for forty years in succession, and the first German newspaper, which an English authority says had 10,000 subscribers. During the middle of the eighteenth century two German newspapers appeared in Philadelphia. The Staatsbote published the first notice of the Declaration of Independence several days before the English papers.

Many Germans and descendants of Germans in the United States have made their mark in the fields of literature, theology, the sciences and the fine arts. The love of Germans for music is proverbial. When they migrated to the new world, music came with them. As early as Christmas, 1743, there was heard in the Moravian Church at Bethlehem, Pa., the sound of violins, flutes and horns, and in the same town Haydn's oratorio, "The Creation," was presented, long before such an attempt was made elsewhere in America. The German song has preserved for the Germans the most sacred memories of their fatherland and is casting rays of sunshine into the somberness of life. If today America is classed among the countries of the world which foster and cherish music, the credit belongs in large measure to those who came

BRUNO PRAGER

Was born in 1868 at Plauen, Germany, and there learned the trade of machinist. In 1892 he came to the United States and for three years was employed in the great plant of R. Hoe & Co., manufacturers of printing presses. His experience gained there gave him his start as a printing press expert. In 1895 Mr. Prager came to New Orleans and started a small shop, which has developed into the present Novelty Machine Works, a large plant with the most modern machinery and tools, located at 472 Howard Avenue. He is a man of wide experience and broad vision, intelligent and conscientious. For many years he has been a valued member and officer of the German Society, and is a member of many social, civic and charitable organizations, as well as a booster for his home city. He married Miss Augusta Koob. They have three children, Hermann, Julius and Augusta.

from the land of Beethoven, Mozart, Bach, Wagner and nearly all the greatest masters in that art.

The first musical instruments in this country were made by Germans. The first pipe organ was built in 1737 by Mathias Zimmermann, in Philadelphia. Three-fourths of the pianofortes made in this country are made by Germans.

A few of the German-Americans whose names have become famous, besides those already mentioned, are John Jacob Astor, Henry Steinway, manufacturer of pianos; the Rev. Dr. Karl Minnigerode, the pastor of President Jefferson Davis; Carl Schurz, major general, senator and minister of the interior under President Hayes; August Belmont, banker and politician; Eberhard Faber, manufacturer of lead pencils; Thomas Nast, famous cartoonist; the Spreckels and Havemeyer, sugar merchants, and many others.

The Germans During the Civil War

During the Civil War forty-five generals and seven major generals of the Union Army were Germans, the most noted among them being Franz Sigel. But on the Confederate side, also noted Germans rendered conspicuous service. General Karl G. Memminger, of South Carolina, a native of Wurtemberg, was called by Jefferson Davis into his cabinet as minister of finance, and General John A. Wagener, a native of Hanover, defended Fort Walker with 200 German artillerymen against the attack of the Union fleet. The Legislature of South Carolina subsequently passed resolutions commending the bravery he and his artillery battalion had displayed in the fight. What an ardent supporter of the Confederacy General Wagener was, is seen from the following war song, composed by him:

> Arise, arise, with main and might,
>   Sons of the sunny clime!
> Gird on the sword, the sacred fight,
>   The holy hour doth chime.
> Arise, the Northern hosts draw nigh
>   In thundering array!
> Arise, ye brave, let cowards fly;
>   The hero bides the fray.
>
> Strike hard, strike hard, thou noble band,
>   Strike hard with arms of fire;
> Strike hard for God and fatherland,
>   For mother, wife and sire.
> Let thunders roar, let lightning flash,
>   Bold Southerners never fear
> The bayonet's point, the sabre's clash!
>   March on, we'll do and dare.
>
> Bright flowers spring from the hero's grave,
>   The craven finds no rest;
> Thrice cursed the traitor and the knave,
>   The hero thrice be bless'd!
> Then let each noble Southern stand
>   With bold and manly eye;
> We'll do for God and fatherland,
>   We'll do, we'll do, or die.

REV. LOUIS VOSS

Rev. Louis Voss, D. D. Born March 7, 1856, in Holstein, Germany. Came to Chicago in 1872. Entered the German Theological Seminary of Newark, N. J., in 1873, and graduated 1879. Took a postgraduate course in Leipzig, 1879 to 1880. Pastor of the First German Presbyterian Church of New Orleans since October, 1880. Editor of the Altenheim Bote 36 years. Sole surviving charter member of the Board of Directors of the German Protestant Home for the Aged. Stated clerk of the Presbytery of New Orleans since 1892, and of the Synod of Louisiana since its organization, 1901. Associate editor of Southwestern Presbyterian for many years. Author of two prize essays on "Eldership" and "Confirmation," "The Beginnings of Presbyterianism in the Southwest," "Louisiana's Invitation to German Settlers," "History of the German Society." In recognition of his literary labors his alma mater conferred on him the degree of Doctor of Divinity in 1913.

A Review of German Immigration

Historically the development of the German element in the United States covers four periods.

Prior to 1700 only individual Germans appear here and there, though even at that time some of them played important parts in the history of the country. During this period the first German, Hans by name, came to Louisiana with La Salle.

From 1700 to 1800 large numbers of Germans located in New York, Pennsylvania and the Carolinas and many of them took part in the Revolutionary War. The first Declaration of Independence was issued in Mecklenburg County, North Carolina, largely inhabited by Germans. The first German colony arrived in Louisiana during the early period of this century.

During the first half of the nineteenth century over a million Germans came to this country. The years 1830 to 1848 were rich in revolutionary movements in Germany, and many of the leaders were exiled, fleeing to this country. Among them were men of the highest intellectual type.

Since 1850 over 3,000,000 Germans have landed in the United States.

The German in America retains an ardent love for his native land and pride in her achievements and strength, but he loves his adopted country better. He may cross the ocean to visit the scenes of his childhood whenever the opportunity offers itself, but not to stay there. When he has satisfied his longing for the old home, he again turns his eyes to the land of the setting sun, the land that received him when he was a stranger or an exile, the land of his children. The German language and customs are dear to him, but he does not regard them as a religion. He appreciates American ideals and quickly adopts the language and customs of the country. He discharges all the duties of citizenship, but maintains the independence of his views. Politicians have long since discovered that they must take the German vote into consideration if they would win, but also that the German vote is a negligible quantity, because the German is an independent thinker and seldom obeys the party lash.

Of late years the character of the immigrants coming to this country has undergone great changes. The arrival of Germans, Irish, Scandinavians and other peoples of north Europe has gradually diminished and their places are now taken by immigrants from the south of Europe. As long as the great mass of immigrants came from north Europe no voice was raised against the new-comers, but since the tide comes mainly from Italy, Austria-Hungary, Russia and the smaller countries in the south of Europe, we begin to realize the danger threatening our institutions and our society from anarchists and criminals of the Black Hand type, the vicious and the depraved, the paupers and the illiterates. How to exclude these undesirable elements is, indeed, a problem which taxes our best legislative wisdom.

For, clearly, a distinction should be made between the worthy and

CHARLES FRANCIS BUCK

Charles Francis Buck was born in Durrheim, Germany, November 5, 1841. His father, burgomaster of the village, having become involved in the Revolution of 1848, emigrated with his family to America in 1852. They landed at New Orleans, where all except Charles and a young sister fell victims to the yellow fever epidemic of 1853. The boy was taken into the home of a fellow countryman, for whom he worked without schooling until 1857. The principal of the Fisk School prepared him for the High School. Graduating from there in 1861, he was elected a beneficiary cadet to the Louisiana State University. Later he studied law, and soon rising to the head of his profession, became widely known in public service and as an orator. Mr. Buck was twice elected City Attorney, and served one term as Representative to Congress. For a number of years he was a member of the Orleans Parish School Board, and from 1880 to the time of his death was president of the German Protestant Orphan Asylum.

Mr. Buck was a Mason of great prominence, being third in point of seniority in the order of Scottish Rite Masons. He died on January 19, 1918, regarded universally as one of the foremost citizens of New Orleans, loved and honored throughout the State.

the unworthy immigrant. Only prejudice can indulge in race hatred. Every race has produced worthy and noble characters. The races of southern Europe have produced some of the highest types of intellectual and moral worth. Italy produced Raphael, the painter; Dante, the poet, and Savanarola, the reformer. The Slav race gave to the world Copernicus, before England produced a Newton, and a Huss, before Germany gave to the world a Martin Luther. To be sure, there is a vast difference between the immigrants and those great names, but so long as personal disqualifications do not debar them they should not be excluded on account of national or racial origin. Many of them become quickly Americanized, and if the parents are not, certainly their children will be, with our system of free secular education in our public schools. We must educate or perish. The Jewish writer, Zangwill, speaks very strikingly of America as a "great melting pot," "God's crucible," wherein all the races of Europe are to be fused and reformed to produce "the American."

It may become necessary to forbid the immigration of illiterates as well as paupers. As to criminals, there can be but one opinion. They are already prevented from landing, and if they have slipped in can be expelled whenever discovered. But let America continue to be the refuge of the oppressed in all the earth, provided they are intelligent, moral and able-bodied and will aid in developing our resources and contribute to our welfare. America, and especially Louisiana, still needs many thousands of strong arms to cultivate the soil and build the railroads and levees and active brains to develop her national treasures in soil and mine and forest.

On the principle enunciated by Solomon in Proverbs 27:2, "Let another man praise thee, and not thine own mouth; a stranger, and not thine own lips," we will let "a stranger" speak who is not of German blood, the Hon. C. A. Newton, Congressman of Missouri. In an elaborate address before Congress, entitled "German Pilgrim Fathers," which we reproduce in part, he gave a review of the share which German immigrants and settlers have had in the development of the United States and a glowing appreciation of its value.

GERMAN PILGRIM FATHERS

By HON. C. A. NEWTON, Congressman of Missouri.

Our writers have had much to say of the landing of the Pilgrims at Plymouth in 1620, but there transpired in the autumn of 1683 an event of equal importance in the making of American history and in the molding of American liberty. The event was the landing of the "Concordia," carrying 13 German families from Crefeld, under the leadership of Franz Daniel Pastorius.

These 13 families established the first German settlement in the

ADOLPH GUSTAVE RICKS

Adolph Gustave Ricks was born September 21, 1842, in the Province of Nassau, Germany. At a very tender age he came with his parents to New Orleans.

His first employment was in Paris, Texas, with an employer who took a personal interest in him. It was there that he received his first schooling in America. When he grew older, he engaged in the dry goods business in Baton Rouge, and later in the hide business in New Orleans, just after his service in the Confederacy. For a half century he was identified with the firm of A. G. Ricks & Co., in the leather business. He was appointed by the court as receiver of the New Orleans Brewing Association, and succeeding that, he was elected president of the Metropolitan Bank. He was elected by the people of New Orleans as a member of the First Commission Council, and served eight years as Commissioner of Finance.

Throughout all of his life, he was identified with every movement for the benefit of the German colony, and was a member, at the time of his death, of the German Society of New Orleans.

He died in New Orleans, in his eighty-fourth year, on December 15, 1925.

United States at Germantown, Pa.   Others followed until many German settlements were established in New York, Pennsylvania, Virginia and Carolina, and no historian can record truthfully the hardships and privations of the early colonies without dealing at great length with the courage, valor and chivalry of the German pioneers of that time.

These German settlers not only did their full share in clearing the forests, navigating the rivers, fighting the Indians, building homes, and establishing schools in our early colonial days, but they contributed extensively to the trades, avocations and industries which developed among the colonies.

The first book on education produced in America was written by Christoph Dock, in 1754, and the first kindergarten was brought to this country in 1826 by Frederick Rapp.   William Rittenhaus erected the first paper mill in this country in 1690, and Thomas Ruetter founded the first iron works in Pennsylvania in 1716.   Kaspar Wuester founded the first glass factory in America in 1739.   Thomas Leiper laid the tracks of the first railroad in America in 1806.

Not only did the early German settlers who came to this country bring with them a determination to clear the fields and establish a civilization which would serve as an asylum for the oppressed, they came with a will to help build a government which would serve as an example of liberty for the Old World, and they brought with them and cherished as sacred the principles of freedom.   It was the German Society of Friends in Germantown, Pa., who, on the 18th of April, 1688, issued the first public protest against human slavery, and of these sainted patriots John Greenleaf Whittier wrote:

> That bold-hearted yeomanry, honest and true,
> Who, haters of fraud, gave to labor its due;
> Whose fathers of old sang in concert with thine,
> On the banks of Swatara the songs of the Rhine,
> The German-born pilgrims, who first dared to brave
> The scorn of the proud in the cause of the slave.

In the early days of our colonial history groups of white settlers, pioneers of American history, battled against privation and savagery in their respective colonies, while they suffered oppression enforced by emissaries from the Old World.   Each colony fought its own battles independent of the other.   There was a lack of that co-operation and concerted action essential to the common welfare.   It remained for a German, Jacob Leisler, Governor of New York, to call together, in 1690, the first successful struggle for American liberty and independence.   For it was the Colonial Congress which unified the forces of all the colonies and made it possible for them to throw their unified strength against the common enemy—Great Britain.

The Germans During the Struggle for American Independence

Between the settlement of Germantown in 1683 and the breaking out of the Revolution in 1776, a multitude of German settlers came among the Colonies.   As the rule of Great Britain became more and

SIGMUND ODENHEIMER

Born in Odenheim, Baden. Was president of the Louisiana German-American *Staats-Verband* up to the time of the war. Member of the German Society. Member of the Turnverein. Member of the Harugari Maennerchor. President of the Lane Cotton Mills Company. President of the New Orleans Permanent International Trade Exhibition.

more oppressive, British influence was asserted with greater force among the English colonists to prevent a rebellion. So great was this influence that Pennsylvania hesitated to join with the other Colonies in their stand for American freedom and independence. It was at this crisis that the German settlers, having no sympathy for the British Crown, threw their weight into the balance and swung the Keystone State into line. And, likewise, the German settlers throughout the Colonies, imbued with the spirit of liberty and fired with a zeal for freedom, stood steadfast for the American cause. British influence in Georgia was so strong that the colony for a time considered separating from the Independence Union and remaining loyal to Great Britain. History records that it was the influence of liberty-loving Germans among the population of that State which finally resulted in Georgia casting her lot with the Colonies in the battle for independence, and it was a German—John Adam Truetlen—who became the Revolutionary Governor of Georgia.

So marked was this evidence of German enthusiasm for the cause of independence that John Dickinson, one of the signers of the Declaration of Independence, wrote in 1775:

"It is amazing to see the spirit of the Germans among us. They speak with infinite pleasure of sacrificing their lives and property for the preservation of liberty, which they know full well how to value, from its deprivation by despotic princes."

It was but natural that Germans in America should be devoted to the cause of freedom. They had come from a land where they had felt the cruel hand of the oppressor, and in this country they had fought the savages and wild beasts, cleared the forests, built their homes, and claimed the soil upon which their battles had been won. Furthermore, they had no royal British connections, they had no prospects of returning to England for political or social preferment, and they owned no estates or gifts from the crown.

In 1775 George Washington was commissioned commander-in-chief of an army to be raised by the Continental Congress, and on June 4 that year Congress issued a call for troops. Pennsylvania forthwith raised four companies of German sharpshooters. They were backwoods pioneers, strong and brave, who had lived among dangers. Under the leadership of Colonel Nagel and Colonel Daudel they started a march of 600 miles to join their commander-in-chief. In large letters upon each man's breast was written "Liberty or Death," and history relates that when these sun-burnt German backwoodsmen arrived at Washington's headquarters, in less than a month after the call for troops went out, tears streamed down his face as he greeted them.

During the siege of Boston these German sharpshooters fired with such deadly aim that when a report of the battle reached London a member of Parliament cried:

"Those Americans know more of our army than we dream of. They shoot it up, besiege, destroy, and crush it, and wherever our officers show their noses they are swept away by American rifles."

CONRAD KOLB

Mr. Kolb was born in Bavaria, in 1874, and educated in public and commercial schools. Upon reaching this country he was engaged in the retail and wholesale delicatessen and grocery business until 1890, when he removed to New Orleans, which has since been his home. Here he became connected with the establishment formerly operated by Mr. Val Merz, which five years later he acquired and has since operated with such success that it is today a nationally known restaurant and eagerly inquired for by visitors. His farm, situated on Gentilly Road, has become a model. He is a member of the various commercial associations, and is always active in the advancement and beautification of his adopted city. Mr. Kolb has always taken interest in the various German singing and other societies. He may well be proud of his achievements.

That the valor and courage of these German soldiers was recognized by the Continental Congress is shown by the fact that on May 25, 1776, Congress authorized the formation of an entire German battalion, one-half to come from Pennsylvania and one-half from Maryland, and so well did they respond that the battalion was quickly over-filled.

General Nicholas Herkimer

During the summer of 1777 the cause of the Revolution was dragging and the condition in the North seemed desperate. General Burgoyne began his famous march from Canada to New York, along the Hudson, with a view to cutting off New England from the rest of the Colonies. With this accomplished, the American cause would be lost. Burgoyne was to be met by a British expedition coming up the Hudson, while Colonel St. Leger was to come from the West, subdue the Mohawk Valley, rob the farmers of their rich harvests, secure abundant supplies, and join Burgoyne at Albany. St. Leger's army of 1,600 men consisted of British regulars, Canadian volunteers, Hessian Chasseurs, and Indians.

Nicholas Herkimer, hearing of St. Leger's approach, raised a force of 800 men, consisting almost entirely of German farmers of the valley. At Oriskany, near the present city of Rome, N. Y., they met in battle. Historians tell us that in proportion to the number engaged it was the bloodiest battle of the war. The two forces came together in a narrow defile. A thunderstorm raged and the rain came down in torrents, so that their old flintlocks could not be used. The battle was fought out with cold steel in a terrible hand-to-hand conflict. No prisoners were taken; all who were lost on either side were slain. But the German farmers, though outnumbered two to one, proved their ability to successfully grapple with these British regulars, Canadians, Hessians and Indians.

St. Leger was defeated and his defeat resulted in the defeat of Burgoyne's entire expedition. The colonies were thrilled by the courage and valor of these German farmers, and Harold Frederick wrote.

"All honor and glory to the rude, unlettered, great-souled yeomen of the Mohawk Valley, who braved death in the wildwood gulch at Oriskany that Congress and the free Colonies might live."

Of the achievement of these German soldiers and their fearless leaders, George Washington said:

"It was Herkimer who first relieved the gloomy scene of the northern campaign. The pure-minded hero of the Mohawk Valley served from love of country and not for reward. He did not want a continental command nor continental money."

Thus it will be observed that Lexington and Concord were not the only fields where embattled farmers stood and resisted British regulars or fired the shot that was heard around the world.

Pastor Mühlenberg

During the dark days immediately before the Revolution, when

RUDOLPH KRAUSE

Rudolph Krause was born in Schlawe, Prussia, June 26, 1863, son of Rudolph and Auguste (Kuehn) Krause. He received his education in the public schools of Schlawe and Coeslin, came to America in 1881 and settled at Jersey City, N. J. He began his business career in 1890 as bookkeeper and assistant treasurer of the Perkins & Muller Lumber Co., of Westlake, La. With Wm. H. Managan, he gradually acquired all the stock of the company. In 1906 the name of the corporation was changed to the Krause & Managan Lumber Co., Ltd., of which he is president. He is also connected with various other industrial, commercial and financial enterprises, is vice-president of the First National Bank of Lake Charles, president of Lake Charles Trust and Savings Bank and vice-president of Murray-Brooks Hardware Co., Lake Charles, and director of numerous financial enterprises in Louisiana.

patriotic hearts were aching under the ever tyrannical grip of George the Third, a Lutheran Church stood at Woodstock, in the Shenandoah Valley. Its pastor was Peter Mühlenberg, whose father was Rev. Heinrich Mühlenberg, the founder of the Lutheran Church in America. Young Mühlenberg was intensely patriotic. He was an intimate friend of George Washington and a co-worker with Patrick Henry. When the war broke he announced that he would preach his last sermon on the following Sunday. This news brought an enormous congregation. Wrapped in his clerical robes, he stood before his vast audience and delivered a farewell sermon which was marked by its fervor. After discoursing for a time upon the wrongs which the Colonies had suffered he exclaimed:

"There is a time for preaching and praying. But there is also a time for fighting, and that time has come now."

Whereupon he threw off his clerical robe and stood forth a soldier in the full uniform of a colonel in the Continental Army. Enthusiasm reigned, and almost the entire congregation enlisted and served with him until the battle for independence was won. So thrilling was the scene of Reverend Mühlenberg's leaving the pulpit to lead a patriotic band to battle for liberty that Thomas Buchanan Read wrote of him:

> Then from his patriot tongue of flame
> The startling words of freedom came.
> And grasping in his nervous hand
> Th' imaginary battle brand,
> In face of death he dared to fling
> Defiance to a tyrant king.

Early in the Revolution Tories and British sympathizers were numerous everywhere. Many were hesitating and some actually opposing the war. When Washington won the Battle of Trenton it was the pastors of the German Lutheran Churches who announced the glad tidings to their congregations, and they used these words:

"But the Lord of Hosts heard the cry of the distressed and sent an angel for their deliverance."

And the patriotic Germans offered prayers and thanksgiving.

Washington's German Body Guard

Treachery and disloyalty were so prevalent among the Colonies that it found its way into the Army and even into Washington's bodyguard, where plots were revealed by which the commander in chief was to be seized and turned over to the British forces. In the solution of this problem will be found the best example of Washington's faith in the patriotism and loyalty of the Germans during our war for independence. Washington abolished his guard and formed a new one made up of 150 Germans, commanded by Col. Jacob Meytinger, Maj. Bartholomaeus von Heer, and Lieuts. Philip Struebing and Johann Nutter. This bodyguard, selected entirely from German stock, guarded the Father of his Country safely through seven years of war, and when the work was finished he selected twelve of these men, who had served

ALBERT WEIBLEN

Born November 9, 1857, in Metzingen, Württemberg, Served his apprenticeship in Stuttgart. Emigrated to America in 1883. After working in different cities he started business on a very small scale and grew with the city. Is engaged in the manufacturing of marble, granite and other stones for building and monumental work. Is president of the Albert Weiblen Marble and Granite Company, also president of the Stone Mountain Granite Corporation, which is a subsidiary. Has built many monuments, mausoleums, fountains, altars and carried out large contracts for the stone and marble work of great buildings and bridges. He is entrusted with the carving of the great Stone Mountain Memorial, near Atlanta, Ga., and the Stone Mountain Granite Corporation is now engaged in this work. He has two sons; the eldest, John Weiblen, is manager of the New Orleans Plant, and his other son, George Weiblen, is manager at Stone Mountain.

longer than any other in the Continental Army, to escort him to his home at Mount Vernon.

General von Steuben

Perhaps the darkest hours of the Revolution were those spent during the winter at Valley Forge. Forlorn, hungry American soldiers left their blood-stained footprints upon the frozen ground while they watched the British Army comfortably encamped in Philadelphia, and while Washington went into the forest to pray for divine help and guidance. The troops had been defeated at Brandywine and Germantown. Philadelphia had been captured by the British, who also held control of the Delaware River, and the entire American Army consisted of less than 5,000 discouraged men. Washington and his soldiers were not trained in military tactics. They were skillful in fighting Indians from ambush, but they did not know how to meet British regulars in the open. Their great need was a general to train the soldiers and their officers in modern civilized warfare in order that during the following season they could meet the seasoned British soldiers in open conflict. While gloom prevailed during the early winter at Valley Forge, Benjamin Franklin was in Europe seeking friends and supplies for the American cause, and he met Friedrich Wilhelm von Steuben, a descendant of a noble military family of Prussia, and who had been reared in the rigorous military school of Frederick the Great. He had taken active part in many battles of the Seven Years' War, and had become an officer of distinction, schooled in the science of modern warfare. During his interview with Franklin he became interested in the American cause, and proceeded at once to this country. Upon his arrival in Boston he addressed a letter to the Continental Congress which read as follows:

"Honorable Gentlemen: The honor of serving a nation engaged in defending its rights and liberties was the only motive that brought me to this continent. I ask neither riches nor title. I am come here from the remotest end of Germany at my own expense, and have given up honorable and lucrative rank. I have made no condition with your deputies in Europe, nor shall I make any with you. My only ambition is to serve you as a volunteer, to deserve the confidence of your general in chief, and to follow him in all his operations, as I have done during the seven campaigns with the King of Prussia. Two and twenty years spent in such a school seem to give me the right of thinking myself among the number of experienced officers, and if I am possessed of the acquirements in the art of war, they will be more prized by me if I can employ them in the service of a Republic, such as I hope to see America soon. I should willingly purchase at the expense of my blood the honor of having my name enrolled among those of the defenders of your liberty."

Congress, thrilled by the unselfish motives which actuated this distinguished soldier to come and battle for the cause of liberty, immediately accepted his services, and he proceeded to the gloomy headquarters at Valley Forge, where Washington appointed him inspector

RUDOLF S. HECHT

Rudolf S. Hecht, president of the Hibernia Bank and Trust Company, New Orleans, was born on June 3, 1885, in Ansbach, Germany. In 1903 he came to the United States to study American banking methods. In the fall of 1906 he came to New Orleans and has been a resident of the city ever since. Step by step he rose, as a result of marked ability. He is actively interested in the educational and other activities of the various bankers' associations. In his own community he fills a position of great influence and authority and is recognized as a leader in all civic and business movements.

He is a life member of the Board of Liquidation of the City Debt, a member of the Board of Port Commissioners and president of the newly organized Public Service Company, Inc.

He is vice president of the Union Indemnity Company of New Orleans, a director in the Federal Reserve Bank of New Orleans, a director of the Mississippi Shipping Company, director in the Jahncke Dry Docks, Inc., D. H. Holmes Co., and Wesson Oil and Snowdrift Co.

He is a member of the Pickwick, Metairie and Country Clubs. He was married in 1911 to Lynne Watkins, daughter of the late Supreme Court Justice Linn Boyd Watkins. They have two daughters, Lynne Paxton Hecht, born in 1914, and Dorothy Watkins Hecht, born in 1925.

general of the Army. He at once set about his task of training and disciplining a heartsore, weary, discouraged army. He brought order out of chaos. He trained the officers in military tactics and drilled the men. He inspired them with hope and renewed courage, and so well did he succeed that when the conflict was renewed with the coming of spring the British were astounded at the force and training of the new army which they encountered.

To tell of all the achievements of that great soldier in that eventful war would take more time than I have allotted to me. Not only did he discipline and train our soldiers, but he distinguished himself as a skillful general in action. At Yorktown he was the only American officer who had been present at a siege. He was in command of a division, and fortune willed that his division should be in the trenches when the first overtures for surrender were made. He had the privilege, therefore, of being in command when the enemy's flag was lowered, and none was more deserving of this great distinction that he.

Of his wonderful services Alexander Hamilton said:

"He benefited the country of his adoption by introducing into the Army a regular formation of exact discipline and by establishing a spirit of order and economy in the interior administration of the regiments."

The writers of American history have had much to say about the valor and chivalry of La Fayette; nor would I detract from the luster of his magnificent service to our country. I do not believe, however, that his achievements for American Liberty were comparable with those of General Baron von Steuben. Nor do I believe that Washington thought they were. As proof of this assertion, I beg leave to call your attention to the last official act of General Washington as Commander in Chief of the American Army, when he wrote to General von Steuben as follows:

"My Dear Baron: Although I have taken frequent opportunities, both in public and private, of acknowledging your great zeal, attention and abilities in performing the duties of your office, yet I wish to make use of this last moment of my public life to signify in the strongest terms my entire approbation of your conduct, and to express my sense of obligations the public is under to you for your faithful and meritorious services.

"I beg you will be convinced, my dear sir, that I should rejoice if it could ever be in my power to serve you, more especially than by expressions of regard and affection; but in the meantime I am persuaded you will not be displeased with this farewell token of my sincere friendship and esteem for you.

"This is the last letter I shall write while I continue in the service of my country. The hour of my resignation is fixed at 1 today, after which I shall become a private citizen on the banks of the Potomac, where I shall be glad to embrace you and testify the great esteem and consideration with which I am, my dear Baron, etc.

"George Washington,
"Commander in Chief, United States Army."

CHARLES WIRTH

Charles Wirth was born March 29, 1851, in Freudenstadt, Württemberg, and landed March 28, 1866, at New Orleans. He was a prosperous and successful merchant and citizen. He retired from business some four years ago. He has been president of the German Protestant Orphan Asylum for many years and still holds this office. He represented the Twelfth Ward in the City Council during Mayor Flower's administration.

What greater evidence could the Father of his Country have displayed not only of his gratitude of German stock but of his conviction that General von Steuben had rendered a service of first importance? If Washington believed that the services of La Fayette were more valuable than those of General von Steuben, then why did he devote the last sacred hour of his military career to writing a letter to him?

General von Kalb

Another German patriot who had the courage to come and fight for American freedom was Johann von Kalb, who was born in Bavaria and who fought the Seven Years' War. He came to this country with La Fayette in 1777. Washington made him a major general in the Continental Army, and for three years he led and fought for our liberty. He was regarded as one of the most experienced, calculating and cautious officers of the whole Army. In the Battle of Camden, riddled with bullets, he fell. When another officer came to assist him, he said:

"This is nothing. I am dying the death I have longed for. I am dying for a country fighting for justice and for liberty."

Christopher Ludwig

Another inspiring figure of German stock who made his contribution to the War of Independence was Christopher Ludwig, a Philadelphia baker, who was made superintendent and director of baking for the entire Army. He was required by the Continental authorities to furnish 100 pounds of bread for every 100 pounds of flour, but he said:

"No; Christopher Ludwig does not wish to get rich by the war. Out of 100 pounds of flour one gets 135 pounds of bread, and so many will I give."

Would to God we had had some Christopher Ludwigs during the World War.

Three of the most important positions in the Continental Army were held by Germans. General von Steuben was Inspector General, and the value of his services I have discussed; General George Weeden, whose real name was Gerhard von der Weiden, was born in Hanover, Germany, and was Quartermaster General of the Army; and Christopher Ludwig was superintendent and director of baking and performed efficiently and well the important task of supplying bread to the Continental soldiers.

Mollie Pitcher

What patriotic American has not been thrilled by the story of Molly Pitcher, whose real name was Marie Ludwig, an American woman of German stock, the wife of a German-American soldier of the Continental Army? For seven long years she went with her husband to the field of battle. She won the name by which she is known in history from the pitcher in which she carried water among flying shot

PETER BLAISE

Born in Freymuig, Alsace-Lorraine, March 19, 1838. On coming to New Orleans, Mr. Blaise identified himself with the beer industry, and was the first to introduce lager beer at the old Southern Brewery. He founded the old New Hope Brewery, on South Prieur street, the first steam brewery in this city; was one of the organizers of the New Orleans Brewing Association and the Standard Brewing Company, of which he was president when he retired from active life. Mr. Blaise died October 4, 1910, aged 72 years.

Notwithstanding his business demands, Mr. Blaise always found time to identify himself with many social and benevolent organizations and among them there was none he prized more higly in his associations than the German Society, of which he was vice president at the time of his death.

Mr. Blaise was married to Miss Josephine Hauck, of this city, who died July 15, 1918. Mr. Blaise is survived by his sons, George P. Blaise and Alphonse Blaise.

and shell to relieve the parched lips of the wounded and dying soldiers. Her husband was an artillery gunner, and when he fell in the heat of the fray at Monmouth it was Molly who sprang to his cannon and with the skill of a veteran hurled destruction into the ranks of the British until reinforcements came.   Washington himself witnessed her act of heroism, and after the war, upon his recommendation, Congress gave her a pension for life.

After American independence was established, Americans of German stock, joined by immigrants from the fatherland, carried the banner of American civilization beyond the boundaries of the original thirteen Colonies and into Kentucky, Indiana, Ohio, Michigan, Wisconsin, Iowa, Missouri, Texas, Colorado, and to the west coast States, and as God-fearing pioneers, Indian fighters and settlers they blazed the trail, which was followed by the clearing of fields, the building of cities, the establishment of schools, the development of industry and commerce, and this continued until 1848, when the failure of the German revolution brought a large number of highly cultured and refined Germans to this country, men of the type of Carl Schurz and others.

Saving the Union

Not only were the German Quakers of Germantown, Pa., almost a century before the Revolution, the first to voice a public protest against slavery, but when the Civil War came two centuries later the German Turners of Washington were the first to enlist in the Army for the defense and preservation of the Union, and three days after Lincoln's call 1,200 Germans in Cincinnati were under arms and ready to march, and during that great conflict 52 Americans of German stock, composed of men like Carl Schurz, Franz Sigel, Adolph von Steinwehr, and Ludwig Blanker, because of their valor and chivalry attained the rank of general in the Union Army.

The achievement of these soldiers of German stock, as well as our generals and officers who fought in defense of the Union during that frightful conflict, are too numerous to mention within the time allotted to me, but I cannot refrain, however, from referring to the marvelous services rendered to the Union by the Germans of St. Louis.

The United States arsenal, containing valuable stores of arms and ammunition, was stationed there.   Missouri was overwhelmingly secessionist, with a governor from the South, who adhered to the same views. His attitude was made fully apparent in his reply to Lincoln's call for volunteers, in which he said:

"Your requisition, in my judgment, is illegal, unconstitutional and revolutionary in its objects, inhuman and diabolical, and cannot be complied with.   Not one man will the State of Missouri furnish to carry on such an unholy crusade."

Not only did Governor Jackson send this insulting and disloyal letter to the President of the United States, but he sent an autographed letter to the president of the Confederacy, requesting him to furnish

PASTOR KOELLE

Rev. Ferdinand Otto Koelle was born in Elberfeld, Germany, on April 19, 1839, and died in New Orleans, October 28, 1904. He was educated for the ministry in Switzerland and came to New Orleans in October, 1868. In April, 1869, he was called to the pastorate of the Second German Presbyterian Church (now Claiborne Avenue Presbyterian Church), corner Claiborne avenue and Allen Street. This was his life work, serving this church to the day of his death. Pastor Koelle was the organizer and first president of the Protestant Home for the Aged, on Magazine and Eleonore streets. He later founded the Protestant Bethany Home, corner Claiborne Avenue and Allen Street. Both of these institutions and also his beloved church are lasting monuments to his energy and zeal.

officers, siege guns and mortars with which to capture the United States arsenal at St. Louis, with its supplies and ammunition, for the use of the South.

Realizing the value to the Confederacy of the military supplies in the arsenal, and with a view to their capture, Governor Jackson had assembled the Missouri militia at Camp Jackson, in St. Louis, under pretext of inspection and drill. Captain Lyon, of the regular army, commanded a small garrison at the arsenal. Understanding the governor's purpose and realizing the importance of saving the arsenal, with its supplies, the Germans of St. Louis rallied overnight to the Turner halls, and within twenty-four hours four regiments were formed, commanded by Blair, Heinrich, Franz Sigel and Colonel Schutter, and on the following morning, May 10, 1861, they marched out, surrounded and captured the rebel Camp Jackson. They forced the governor to flee for his life, and they saved Missouri to the Union.

The value to the Union of this achievement wrought by the Germans of St. Louis cannot be overestimated. It was a crucial point in the war, and but for this success the history of the war might have been different. The recapture of St. Louis would have been a difficult task for the Union Army, and the children in our schools today would probably be reading of the siege of St. Louis instead of the siege of Vicksburg.

Barbara Fritchie

Who has not been thrilled by the story of Barbara Fritchie, a German woman, whose maiden name was Hauser, and who was immortalized by John Greenleaf Whittier. Born before the Revolution, she was past 90 years of age when the Civil War came. She lived at Frederick, Md. Stonewall Jackson, with an army of Confederate soldiers, came to town. Every Union flag was lowered, save one. Out of an attic window, past which Jackson's army had to go, floated the Stars and Stripes of Barbara Fritchie. The Confederates shot it down. The fires of patriotism kindled within her, and I will let John Greenleaf Whittier tell you what she did:

> Quick, as it fell, from the broken staff
> Dame Barbara snatched the silken scarf.
> She leaned far out on the window sill,
> And shot it forth with a royal will.
> "Shoot, if you must, this old gray head,
> But spare your country's flag," she said.

Germans During the World War

The real test of the patriotism of Americans of German blood came with the World War. It is but natural that they should have regarded with sorrow and regret a conflict which made it necessary for them to fight against their kinsmen in the land from which they came, or from which their fathers came. They are a people with strong family

REV. LUDWIG P. HEINTZ

Came to this country in his early manhood and resided in New Orleans for fifty-one years. He was a profound student. In 1864 he was called to take charge of the German Evangelical Protestant Church, corner Philip and Chippewa streets, which in 1875, under his direction, erected the large edifice corner Jackson Avenue and Chippewa street. Here he devoted himself until his death to the welfare of his people. In 1866 he organized the German Protestant Orphan Asylum, whose inmates regarded him as their father. In 1858 he was instrumental in founding the Humbolt Lodge, F. and A. M., and at the same time established the Rose Croix Chapter. Later he was identified with the Kosmos Lodge No. 171, A. A. S. R., which conducted their meetings in the German language. He held the position of auditor until his life career ended, in December, 1901.

and country ties, and it is but human that they should grieve at the prospect of such a conflict.

And yet, when the call to arms came, the Germans responded without faltering, and so valiantly did they fight that every casualty list from the American front contained a substantial number of German names. It may have been a bitter duty for them, but it has been said, and well said, too, that a "bitter duty well performed is the best test of patriotism."

I have the honor to represent in Congress a district containing more than a half million people. A vast majority of that population is of German stock. Detectives and secret service men from Washington kept those people under continual surveillance, and yet, during the World War, in that entire district, not one American of German blood was convicted for disloyalty.

Not only is the military record of Americans of German stock who fought for the defense of our country an enviable one, but their achievements in civil life have never been surpassed. In agriculture, industry and commerce, they have done their full share toward developing the resources and creating the wealth of the Nation. Their turnvereins and gymnastic societies have done much to develop the physical man and womanhood of the country, and it is through their influence mainly that athletic departments have been established in the schools and universities of the Nation. They have made large contributions to our arts and sciences and their symphony orchestras and singing societies have greatly added to the character, culture and happiness of our people.

Not only should we turn the alien property, or its full equivalent in value, back to the people to whom it belongs, because we cannot do less with honor, but should we not, out of consideration for the feelings of more than 25,000,000 of our citizens who come from German stock—citizens who have contributed so much toward the development and defense of our country—should we not for their sake do justice to their kinsmen on the other side?

What other race which has contributed to the melting pot from which comes the free people of this great Republic can boast of a greater contribution to the establishment and maintenance of our liberties or to the building of our institutions? What race has a better right to sing, "Land where our fathers died," or in the words of Frederick Lucien Hausmer:

> Oh, beautiful our country,
> Round thee in love we draw.
> For thee our fathers suffered;
> For thee they toiled and prayed;
> And upon thy holy altars
> Their willing lives they laid.

FRITZ JAHNCKE

Fritz Jahncke was born at Hamburg, Germany, in 1848. He served in the Franco-Prussian War and at its close came to New Orleans. Shortly after his arrival he started in a modest way in the business which at present has grown into a large and important corporation. He started with nothing, and while accumulating a large fortune, also gained a reputation for honesty and integrity, which he valued more than riches. In financial and business transactions his maxim was "to do the right thing at all times and do it well." He was throrough in everything, so that the name of "Jahncke" in a business way was the equivalent to a trade mark of recognized dignity and standing. He was straight forward and reliable in all the relations of life.

In 1876 Mr. Jahncke married Miss Margaret Lee. This union was blessed with three splendid sons, who are all living today—captains of industry.

WHAT GERMANS HAVE CONTRIBUTED TO OUR NATIONAL LIFE

BY PHILIP VOLLMER, Ph. D., D. D.

The American nation may be fitly compared to a stately oak tree with many racial roots through which the sap of liberty found its way into the mighty trunk, giving beauty and vitality to branch and leaf, to foliage and fruit. There are five principal roots which constitute the main sources of American civilization—the English, the German, the Dutch, the French-Huguenot and the Scotch-Irish. The following discussion is limited to the amount and quality of the sap which the German root has contributed and is still contributing to this mighty oak.

Large in Numbers

In the first place, the Germans are a most important numerical factor in our national life. German immigration began when, on the 6th of October, 1683, Daniel Pastorius and his company of Mennonites landed at Philadelphia and subsequently founded Germantown. There are now in America over 14,000,000 of people either born abroad or descended from German ancestors. In some States, as in Wisconsin, the Germans are in the majority. New York is the third largest German city in the world. Pennsylvania has always been a banner State of German immigration. It has been asserted and never successfully disproved that three-fifths of the present inhabitants of Pennsylvania have German blood running in their veins. Their present names are not a certain criterion of national descent, because thousands of Germans, some from worthy and others from unworthy motives, have anglicized their names. Scratch a Mr. Carpenter, or a Mr. King, or a Mr. Cook, or a Mr. Taylor, or a Mr. Black, or a Mr. Stone, and you find in many cases a Zimmermann, a Koenig, a Koch, a Schneider, a Schwartz, and a Stein. A German Pennsylvania farmer by the name of Klein recently held a family reunion. His four sons were present and their names had been changed respectively into Kline, Small, Little, and Short. There are today seven hundred thousand people in Pennsylvania speaking that homely and mellow Pennsylvania-German dialect. As the Philadelphia Ledger said recently, "It were a pity if this dialect should soon die out." But there is at present little danger of this, for I know from experience that even negroes, Scotchmen, and people of other nationalities, have been assimilated and become German-Pennsylvanians in speech and customs. Even before the Revolution the Germans were so strong in Pennsylvania, that the question came up in the legislature as to whether the German or the English should be the official language. A tie vote resulted and the president, a German, gave the casting vote in favor of English—a wise decision, I think, all things considered.

OTTO KNOOP

Otto Knoop was one of the oldest prominent dealers in lumber, shingles, sash, doors and blinds in New Orleans. He was born in Holstein, Germany, in 1837, and there educated. He came to this country in 1854, settled in New Orleans and later moved to Stonewall, Miss. He was a ship carpenter by trade and worked at this in the Bayou State. He returned to New Orleans in 1872 and embarked in the present business. He was married in New Orleans in 1873 to Miss Margaret E. Buddig. He was the father of four sons: Otto G., Harry D., Theodore M. and George E., who continue his business under the name of the Otto Knoop Lumber and Realty Co., Ltd., at 1201 Julia street. Socially Mr. Knoop was a Mason, a Knight of Honor and a member of the Clio Street Church. He was a member of the New Orleans German Rifle Club, the German Masonic Benevolent Club, and the German Society of New Orleans. He was a director for about eighteen years of the German Protestant Orphan Asylum, and a director of the German Protestant Home for the Aged and Infirm and of several other organizations.

The Educational Influence

The Germans have been, in the second place, an important educational factor in American literature, science and art. The German's love of education in all its branches is generally conceded. Luther and Zwingli were the founders of the modern public school, Melanchthon is known as the reformer of the German Universities; the Moravian Bishop Comenius, who once received an urgent call to the presidency of Harvard College, was the pathfinder of modern educational methods, and Froebel was the founder of the "Kindergarten." This inborn love for popular and higher education the first German settlers transplanted to America. Franklin, in 1774, reported that they owned six printing presses and were in the habit of importing large quantities of books.

Prof. Hinsdale, in his recent article on "Foreign Influence Upon American Education," says that in 1776 Franklin visited Goettingen to get German ideas to guide him in founding the University of Pennsylvania, and it is well known that those of our American universities which deserve that name are modeled after German and not after English patterns. Professor Hinsdale proceeds as follows: "William Penn, it may be set down as certain, got his ideas of the common school from Germany. The German colonists he brought here represented a far higher level of education than his English colonists. They were more advanced in the arts, they were better versed in letters and they represented a higher educational standard than then existed in England, whose universities and schools were then at their lowest ebb, and even from these Dissenters were excluded."

The Germans in Politics

In the third place, the German Americans have always been an important political factor—not in the sense of office seeking—they never got their fair share in political prominence—but in the sense of intense American patriotism. While the self-respecting German never loses his love for his mother, the old Fatherland, he embraces with all the powers of his soul his young self-chosen bride—America, with as great fervor as a lover embraces the mistress of his affection without neglecting his mother. In times of peace, the German as a rule stood for honesty, political decency and reform. In times of war he was foremost to defend the "Star Spangled Banner." Two years before the Declaration of Independence was signed the German colonists declared for absolute separation from England. When the rumblings of the Revolution became louder, the King of England wanted to know two things; first, how the German colonists stood on the question of Independence, and secondly, whether many of them had been soldiers before they emigrated. The report made his countenance fall! for it stated that the Germans were almost unanimously in favor of independence and that they even had committees of correspondence at work to consolidate the Germans in other colonies.

During the Civil War, 200,000 Germans fought on the side of the

R. J. HOLZER

Union and very few on the side of the Confederacy. An unimpeachable authority has stated: "As between the native born of the North and the native born of the South, independently and alone, the Civil War would almost certainly have terminated differently, if the help of the foreign-born Germans in the North had not been arrayed against the Confederacy."

During the Spanish-American War an American of French descent, Dewey, destroyed the weak fleet at Manilla; an American of German descent, Schley, defeated the much more formidable fleet at Santiago; another American of German descent, Schafter, won the land battle before Santiago, and an American of Dutch descent, Roosevelt, was a leader in the latter battle. But the American of English descent, Sampson, was ten miles away at the most critical hour of the entire Spanish war, yet, Anglo-Saxon like, was quite ready to claim the credit for the victory. Does not this record show the composite character of our nation?

The Germans in Religion

I will only touch briefly on the Germans as a religious factor. The Gospel is the same for all nations, but each nation manifests its power in a different way. The Germans of the different denominations support tens of thousands of churches in America which stand for deep reverence in public worship, for an orderly service with liberty to adapt it to circumstances, for the idea of the church year, for the educational method in propagating the faith as over against the one-sided revival method. The Germans lay great stress on what Dr. Cuthbert Hall recently called the "Hallowing of Education." They do not only acknowledge that there is a difference between instruction and education, but they put the strongest emphasis upon it. Mere instruction is not education. Education is the bringing out of all the faculties of the child, the development of the entire nature, the training of the intellect and the heart and the will—in a word, the whole man. To give all attention to the intelligence of the child and to neglect its religious training is not adequate education. The great crimes against society are not committed by illiterate men, but by people who in their youth were instructed but not educated; by men who grow up from youth to manhood without religious training. Isolated cases are found of violence, robbery and other crimes perpetrated by the ignorant, but the crimes that go to the heart of society and shake it to its very foundations—the frauds on public funds; the robbery of savings banks and insurance offices, by which countless numbers are made to mourn; the unsettling of public credit; the gambling in stocks; the squandering and the pilfering of the treasury of the nation; the unlimited power of corporations, by which the artisan and the laborer may be robbed of the fruits of their honest toil—these and many more such evils are not the work of ignorant and illiterate men.

Thousands of parochial schools are supported by German churches, not for teaching the German language, as some mistakenly suppose

PHILIP D. MAYER

Mr. Mayer was born in Germany in 1841, emigrated in his early youth and settled in New Orleans, where he entered the cigar business. Today one of the largest cigar factories in the South is operated under the name of Phil. D. Mayer & Son, Ltd., and managed by his son, Julius H. C. Mayer. The firm operates two plants, one in New Orleans and one in Donaldsonville, employing between 400 and 500 men and women.

Mr. Mayer was active in all commercial enterprises and German social affairs, having been a member of the Board of the German Protestant Orphan Asylum, as well as the German Society. He also, during his early commercial years, represented the Germania Life Insurance Company. His death occurred in 1907.

(for many are entirely English in language), but in order to give effect to their cherished theory of education.

Lastly, the Germans have been and still are an important social factor, having contributed many beautiful features to the character of this mighty nation. Their "Gemütlichkeit," their high esteem of home life, their aversion to boarding house life, their families, their hospitality, their fondness for music, have become proverbial. The "New Woman" finds no favor with them. Club life is not appreciated.

What Are The Lessons?

From the foregoing discussion three lessons may be learned, the first of which is, that America is **not an Anglo-Saxon nation**, but a composite people. The descendants of the two low-German tribes, the Angles and the Saxons, that emigrated to England (in A. D. 499) are almost extinct even in England, for England's present population is a mixture of Norman, Anglo-Saxon, Danish and Dutch elements, while Scotland, Wales and Ireland are largely Celtic. The leading merchants of England are Scotch and Irish, her leading financiers are Jews, the reigning family is German and her army is recruited principally from Scotch and Irish. To apply, therefore, the glib phrase "Anglo-Saxon," coined by Lord Macaulay, to the American nation when it does not even suit Old England, shows bigotry or ignorance, or both. You cannot truthfully call a civilization by a name that has only a few representatives among it, and which in its essence points to other sources. America may be compared to a great cooking pot, in which a nutritious stew is being prepared. The outcome of it will not be an English stew, although John Bull contributed a respectable piece of beef to it; it will not be an Irish stew; it will not be a German Nudelsuppe. It will be a mixed stew in which the prevailing elements are the English, the German, the Irish, the Dutch and the Scotch—a genuine **American stew**, with a taste and flavor entirely its own; a new creation, unlike all other nations—a harmonious blending of the best features found in all these racial elements. America has a great future!

Much of this Anglo-Saxon talk, emanating chiefly from London, is nothing more than a cleverly concealed attempt to tell us that after all America is nothing more than an English dependency, in its origin, its leading constituents, and its type of civilization. All of which we stoutly deny. This sort of reasoning is an example of the truth of Mr. Froude's dictum, that you can make anything you please of the facts of history, just as you can write any word with the letters of the alphabet, provided you only pick those you want and leave the rest.

Secondly, truth and pride should induce descendants of Germans to keep alive the memory of their forbears in America. To tell the truth about German-Americans is especially necessary since the recent war propaganda. We can discharge this duty by informing our children

HENRY L. FRANTZ

Was born September 3, 1846, in Alsace-Lorraine. His parents emigrated to New Orleans in 1857. He married Miss Johanna Waldo in 1869; she was the daughter of one of the honored and respected Third District families. This union was without issue, although the couple reared six partly orphaned children, and partly reared two more.

Mr. Frantz started in the blacksmith and wagon manufacturing business with a cousin in 1871. In 1874 he associated himself with Mr. Jacob Schoen in the undertaking business. He became a director and president of the Third District Building Association and held the same position in the Third District Bank. He was one of the organizers of the Orleans Manufacturing Co., and its president at the time of his death. He served two terms as a member of the City Council; also several years on the Orleans Levee Board; was one of the organizers of the City Park Commission. He also was one of the organizers of the Bethlehem Orphan Asylum, a member of its board of directors and the vice-president up to the time of his death. This institution both he and his wife remembered generously in their bequests.

JACOB SCHOEN

was born at Eiglach near Worstadt, Hesse Darmstadt, Germany, June 8, 1841. He came to this country in 1859. He was a boss longshoreman and remained in that business for seven years, after which he entered that of an undertaker. He formed a partnership in 1874 with H. L. Frantz who disposed of his share in 1879. Mr. Schoen then took his oldest son Philip into the business under the firm name of Jacob Schoen & Son which existed at the time of his death. His son, P. J. Schoen, Sr., died June 11, 1927, and Mrs. Schoen is continuing the business under the management of her sons Philip J., Jr., Eduard A., and Gerard L. Schoen, representing the third generation.

of the history of German-Americans, by encouraging them to read an article like this, by writing for them a short sketch of their parents' and grandparents' lives, by holding annual banquets on "Forefathers' Day" (October 6, the landing of the "Concordia"), by placing proper literature in the public libraries, etc. A school history, for instance, which makes everything of Plymouth Rock and the "Mayflower" and nothing at all or very little of Germantown and the "Concordia," is imperfect, and the Germans should no longer tamely submit to the present inadequate treatment of the settlement of America in our lower and higher schools. We all honor Penn, Washington, Lincoln, and Garfield; but the descendants of Germans should not be ashamed of Daniel Pastorius, Herkimer, Schlatter, Mühlenberg, Zinzendorf, Sauer, Von Steuben, Gallatin, and Admiral Schley.

Lastly, let us perpetuate the virtues of our German ancestors and cultivate the German language. The knowledge of two languages does not impair American patriotism. Presidents Cleveland and Harrison were not less patriotic because they had a German Fräulein as governess for their children and enjoyed a German Christbaum in the White House under which the little ones sang the beautiful German Christmas carols. At a time when Anglo- and Irish-Americans spend thousands of dollars to acquire the German, those who possess the language should not throw it away. Even if our churches should become English, the educated offspring of German ancestry should cultivate the language of science and philosophy.

What the French Huguenots do in Europe and America; what the Americans of British and Irish and Dutch and Swedish descent do in the United States—form societies and publish literature to show the influence of their stock upon America—this the German-Americans have a right and even a duty to do also. Only let them beware lest politicians use these organizations for their selfish purposes and thus bring disgrace upon the great German-American name, as was so frequently done in the past generation

If the German contribution to the make-up of this nation could be eliminated it would mean a great irreparable loss to our country of whose greatness and power no element is prouder than the Americans of German extraction. But there is no fear of this. Even if we would, we could not get rid of the German factor in our national life, for of the Germans it is true what a poet said:

> "Es kann die Spur von meinen Erdentagen
> Nicht in Aeonen untergeh'n."

RICHARD FROTSCHER

Born at Leipzig, Saxony, on March 15, 1833, and died at New Orleans February 2, 1896. He came to New Orleans at an early age and in 1865 established himself in the Seed business. The name of Richard Frotscher was known to all farmers not only in this State but also throughout the whole South. He was considered an authority on seeds and for many years published "The Southern Garden Manual."

JULIUS KOCH

Was born May 1, 1857, in Stuttgart, Germany, and died in New Orleans on June 1, 1918. He came to America at a youthful age and spent some years in Philadelphia and St. Louis.

Mr. Koch came to New Orleans in 1885 and lived here until his death in 1918. He was considered one of the foremost Architects and Contractors of this City. Mr. Koch was prominent in fraternal and social circles. He was a 32° Mason and Shriner and also took an active part in the many charitable causes undertaken in the City of New Orleans.

THE GERMANS IN LOUISIANA HISTORY— THEIR SPLENDID WORK IN COLONIZATION

By MRS. S. B. ELDER

The following article appeared in the Daily Picayune on October 9, 1911. We cannot fail to appreciate the kindly spirit manifested towards the Germans, in this interesting story, told by that gifted writer. Mrs. Elder. The article is based partly on a book published in 1909 from the pen of Prof. J. Hanno Deiler, Professor Emeritus of Tulane University, elsewhere alluded to in these pages, entitled, "The Settlement of the German Coast of Louisiana and the Creoles of German Descent." Prof. Deiler had retired from active service in Tulane University to devote himself entirely to his literary labors. He spent his summer months in his Tusculum in the beautiful town of Covington, but not in idleness. He revised and elaborated his pamphlet on Louisiana so that it grew from 32 pages, as originally published, to a book of 135 pages, reprinted from German-American Annals, a publication of the German-American Historical Society of Philadelphia. The new material was derived largely from documents in the Marine Archives in Paris, copies of which were made at the request of the Historical Society of Louisiana. With infinite patience Prof. Deiler sifted this material and rescued from oblivion many facts of highest value to the history of the Germans in Louisiana. Prof. Deiler died on July 20, 1909.

In a large number of other pamphlets written in German, like "The German Churches of New Orleans," "History of the German Society of New Orleans " "A Forgotten German Colony," "History of the German Press," "History of the Germans on the Lower Mississippi," "Louisiana, a Home for German Settlers," and others, Prof. Deiler drew a highly interesting picture of the share which Germans have had in the development of this part of the United States.—Note by the Editor.

The very first German on the lower Mississippi of whom we have any historical knowledge was a follower and a friend of the heroic French explorer, Robert de La Salle.

He joined La Salle's expedition in St. Domingo, where, their leader being laid up with fever, many of his dissolute crew abandoned the French ships, and others were engaged to take the place of the deserters. Among the new men was one "Hans," a German, whom the French recorded in their annals as "Heins," and on a map of 1720 a river is found bearing the name "Riviere Heins."

The occasion for thus immortalizing an humble German sailor was as follows: When La Salle's expedition was crossing a river poor Hans fell into the muddy stream and was drawn with great difficulty out of danger. Father Anastasius, a priest accompanying the pioneers,

JACOB HASSINGER

Jacob Hassinger was born in Rehborn, Rhenish Bavaria, in 1828, and emigrated with his parents to America in 1841. Shortly after the arrival of the family, his father died. This threw responsibilities on his young shoulders. He went to work manfully to carry out his obligations and at the same time to educate himself. He became an apprentice printer in the office of the German Gazette, then edited by Joseph Cohn, and later became the owner of the paper. He started the Germania Savings Bank, for the purpose of giving the working people a place to deposit their savings.

G. A. BLAFFER

Gustave Adolphe Blaffer was born in New Orleans on May 22, 1849. He was the son of John Blaffer and Anna Ostermann. He departed this life Feb. 6, 1924.

His early manhood was spent in commercial pursuits, but later he affiliated himself with the Germania Savings Bank, and remained with that institution until its consolidation with the Commercial National Bank. At his death he was the dean of bankers in New Orleans having spent over forty years in the banking business. Ten years before his death he retired from active business, but always took special interest in all affairs of the bank which his energy and ambition had brought to success.

says that: "A German from Wittenburg named Hans got stuck too fast in the mud that he could scarcely get out." La Salle named the river then, all unconscious of the connection which later would exist between the names of Hans and La Salle.

We know that in January, 1687, La Salle made a last desperate attempt to march overland in search of his "lost river," and that seventeen men were selected to accompany him on the journey towards the Mississippi, and if possible in reaching Canada. Hans was one of the seventeen—and this is proof that La Salle thought well of him.

On the 18th of March, 1687, La Salle was killed by Duhaut, a Frenchman who wished to be leader of the expedition. Martin records that "the murderers quarreled among themselves and one was killed." The man killed was Duhaut, and the hand that avenged the murder of La Salle was that of Hans, the German. He had taken the death of his noble leader very much to heart, and punished one crime by another, even desiring to kill Duhaut's accomplice, but Jontel persuaded him from committing this deed.

The returning party numbered eight, but when near the Arkansas River, Hans, fearful of being punished for Duhaut's murder, withdrew from the band and joined the Coenis Indians. He bore with him, at his urgent request, a Latin certificate stating that he was innocent of La Salle's death. What became of him no one knows, but on the first pages, as it were, of Louisiana history, the French and German names are thus intertwined.

There is a marked and wide discrepancy here between Judge Martin and Prof. Deiler's account in regard to our German Hans. The first includes him among the murderers of La Salle, but the professor's almost exhaustive researches reveal a different story—and human nature, unassisted by Christian teachings—made Hans the executioner of a criminal whom no law at that time could reach. We see the same thing done in our own day where justice is at hand for every one, and yet "private" vengeance has its sway.

Why Thousands of Germans Emigrated to Louisiana

They came, just as others may come shortly, because Louisiana's advantages were proclaimed broadcast—even as they are being done at present. But there is a difference. What is stated now is founded on facts. What was stated in 1717, by the Western Company, under the presidency of the famous John Law, was based upon dreams, upon expectations of finding gold and silver and pearls in Louisiana, as the Spanish had done in Mexico. It is true that "the fertility of the soil" was also made a prominent feature of attraction, and yet no attention had been given to agriculture; but the third inducement was the rich revenue to be derived from "trade monopoly." Large land grants were given to wealthy men and women in France, and they were to induce hard-working people to take up these lands. They to "get rich quick" in consequence.

Law himself was given two immense concessions. The larger of

EMILE FERDINAND DEL BONDIO

Emile Ferdinand Del Bondio was born July 16, 1842, in Mainz, Germany, and died May 3, 1904. He arrived in New Orleans at the age of 16. Commenced his business career in the commission house of his brother, Frederick Del Bondio. After the Civil War he established a commission house on his own account at Poydras and South Peters Street. For 25 years he remained at one location, and by superior ability he attained the highest place in the commercial world.

He was a member of several social clubs, director of several banks, also of the former Times-Democrat, and member of several Carnival clubs. He was a man of wonderful executive ability. His sterling qualities of character had gained for him the highest esteem of his associates and friends. His home and family life was ideal. Every one with whom he had any dealings became an admiring friend. His word was his bond; no one was ever found to question his fine sense of honor and his unflinching integrity the two on the lower Arkansas River, and the smaller seven "lieues" below New Orleans. He knew well that land as such could not build up fortunes, but willing and able toilers would make rich returns—and his shrewd mind turned to the thrifty Germans along the Rhine.

Thirty years of war, and Louis XIV's devastation of German provinces, had impoverished and disheartened many an industrious farmer, so these listened to the beautiful promises connected with Louisiana's soil, mineral wealth and unlimited commerce, and left Alsace, Lorraine, Baden, Wurttemberg and even Switzerland to seek fortunes in a new and untried country.

All our early French historians say that 10,000 Germans started for Louisiana.

The sufferings and hardships of those thousands fill one's heart with sorrow—for the sad record reads thus: "Only a small portion of these 10,000 Germans ever reached the shores of Louisiana."

They died in the French ports while waiting for vessels on which to embark. No preparations had been made for their shelter or food or comforts, so that disease broke out among them and laid them low. Others died on the voyage out, as the hardships on crowded shipboard were too severe, and thus sickness and starvation thinned their numbers most cruelly.

Prof. Deiler speaks of "only forty Germans landed in Louisiana out of 200 who had gone aboard."

Martin's history speaks of "only 200 survivors out of 1,200."

Then the pitiful story is told of "very sick Germans," who reached land only to die far away from home. The total number of German immigrants is put down at about 6,000, who left their homes for Louisiana, and of these only about 2,000 were landed in Biloxi and upon Dauphine Island. But the survivors were very different from the early French colonists—many of whom were idle vagabonds of whom some writers add "and you cannot find families of these now in Louisiana."

The Germans were never idle, and they went beyond the city limits and settled within six or seven leagues of New Orleans, and "this part of the coast is the best cultivated and most thickly settled tract of the colony."

The Germans on Law's Arkansas concession fared badly. Law's promises of help in every way did not materialize—and they resolved to return to Europe; but Governor Bienville persuaded them to remain, and gave them rich lands on what is known as the "German coast."

The Germans also formed a large part of the French colonial troops. When their time of service expired they generally settled on land near the German coast. Of these, Governor Kerlerec wrote to France begging that German soldiers be sent to him in place of French ones, "not only on account of their superior discipline and fighting qualities, but because the colonists had as great a dread of the violence, cruelty and debauchery of the troops ordinarily sent out from France, as they had of the savages."

GEORGE JURGENS

Born at Lage, Prussia, December 25, 1850. With his father's permission he landed at Cuba at an early age. He remained there for one year and then came to New Orleans. Dr. F. M. Bonzanno, United States engineer, placed him in charge of a lighthouse down the river. At the age of 19 he was promoted to captain. Returning to New Orleans, he was employed by Frank Roder. After being in his employ for one year, he was taken into the business as a partner. This firm—F. Roder & Co.—were wholesale liquor dealers and sales agents for Sunrise Rice Mill. In 1889 he became sole owner, later on taking Jules C. Koenig as a partner. They remained together for several years until Mr. Jurgens retired from active business. Mr. Jurgens donated a building for the Jurgens Free Kindergarten. He died February 21, 1924, at the age of 73 years.

The first landing of our German colonists was at Biloxi and Dauphine Island—and it is probable that more than a thousand died of starvation and disease on these sandy spots. Yet in spite of death and disaster, the Germans built up the homes and farms found today in the flourishing parishes of St. Charles and St. John the Baptist. This part of the river coast was a howling wilderness when the survivors of the 10,000 spread themselves over the land, which had no levees, no drainage and whose settlers often found their house roofs their only refuge against the annual inundations.

One distressed farmer petitioned the Superior Council to advance him some rice, as his whole year's labor had been swept away in the spring floods, "but if assisted in supporting his family until the next harvest he would pay back the rice thus furnished in his time of need." The prayer was granted the same day it was presented to the Council. Remember, that these industrious, honest toilers had no plows, nor horses, nor oxen, and only a few families owned a cow. Yet with pick-ax, hoe and spade alone, these noble German settlers built up flourishing farms, also schools and churches.

Whatever strong hands and stronger will could do was done. We learn that when uncommonly hard work was spoken of, this remark could be heard: "It takes German people to do that."

They suffered also from Indian foes. Once their terror was so great from Choctaw inroads that they fled from home and fields, leaving these to be destroyed, while they began life anew in locations more protected and adjoining a larger settlement of their compatriots.

It is strange Martin's history gives so little notice of the German settlers. On page 184 he says: "The settlements along the Mississippi, above the city and below, were now in high cultivation." But he does not explain that this condition was due alone to German thrift and unflagging toil.

Laussat, colonial prefect of Louisiana, when writing to France of its newly-regained territory, says: "What is called here the 'German Coast' is the most industrious, the most populous, the most respected part of the inhabitants of this colony."

Here is an opinion worth recording:

As early as 1724 the Germans had a neat little chapel on the right bank of the great river. And this is about the time when Father Charlevoix wrote to a friend in France that the people in New Orleans "had lent the Lord half of a miserable 'store' for divine service, and now they want the Lord to move out again and accept shelter in a tent."

In 1740 the small chapel was replaced by the first Red Church. The name referred to the coat of red paint which made it a landmark for the boats on the Mississippi River. It sounds paradoxical to assert that a very large part of our French inhabitants are Germans. Of course this fact is well known to many of our readers, but a few illustrations may prove interesting:

German names suffered queer changes as they were pronounced by

ANTHONY FREDERICK BULTMAN

Anthony Frederick Bultman was born in New Orleans on January 8, 1853, only child of Magdalena Koehler and Anthony F. Bultman, both of Germany. He received his education in the public schools of this city. As a young man he took up clerical work until he purchased an old established undertaking business from Wm. Feltman, of 2917 Magazine Street. This was forty-five years ago. In experience and years, he is the oldest funeral director in the city of New Orleans. In 1884 he married Miss Ida Maurer, who came to New Orleans with her parents from Germany. To this union ten children were born. Mr. Bultman is still actively engaged in the mortuary profession, as treasurer of the Bultman Mortuary Service, Inc. Associated with him are his two sons, A. Fred Bultman, Jr., president, and Henry J. Bultman, secretary. The business continues to represent the highest ideals and is one of the representative firms in the city.

French tongues, and Prof. Deiler gives one example of transmigration of family names which proves how thoroughly this fine German historian did his work of research and elucidation.

Take, for instance, the family of Jean Zweig, who came to Louisiana in the ship "Les Deux Freres." When the son of Jean Zweig married Suzanna Marchand, the French notary, unable to pronounce the groom's name, asked its meaning. Being told that "Zweig," translated, was "a branch," the French official recorded the name "Zweig," with the addition Labranche, and all Louisianians called "Labranche" are of heroic German ancestry.

Changes because of French pronunciation, or from other reasons, took place in the names of Schants, now Chance; Foerster, now Fortier; Heidel, now Haydel; Traeger, now Tregre; Dubs, now Toups; Klomp, now Klump; Schaf, now Chauffe; Wagensbach, now Waguespack; Trischl, now Triche; Foltz, now Folse; Manz, now Montz; Lesch, now Leche.

These names were all concessionists; that is, they owned land, and employed workers, called "engages," and are recorded in the census of 1721 to 1824.

The names of the "engages" are never given unless they became land owners through their skill and economy.

But the names of our Creole families given above bear out the statement that many of our French citizens are largely Germans—and as such have every reason to be proud of their ancestors, "whose descendants yet remain, ranking among the most industrious, wealthy and enterprising citizens of the State."

It would be well for Louisiana were 10,000 more Germans to settle upon her reclaimed, fertile acres and make them into homes of wealth and beauty. Emigration today is not connected with hardships and sufferings known in early times, and all promises made to new settlers at present should be fulfilled to the very letter, so that no sad stories of disaster or deception may mar the colonization efforts now being made in 1911.

WHAT THE GERMANS HAVE DONE FOR LOUISIANA

This article, written by the Editor of this pamphlet, appeared in The Daily Picayune of Sunday, October 19, 1913. It was illustrated by pictures of C. Roselius, Hon. Martin Behrman, J. Hanno Deiler, A. G. Ricks and Jos. Voegtle.

In an editorial of Sunday, October 5, 1913, on "German Day Celebration," the Picayune remarked:

"About the year 1715 John Law, a Scotchman, and perhaps the most famous speculator and promoter of speculation the world ever

MATHIEU VONDERBANK

Born in Aachen, Germany, February 24, 1842. After spending several years in London, he came to New York in 1866, and in the following year to New Orleans, where he lived till his death. In 1874 he married Miss Babette Oettinger, of Fuerfeld, Wurttemberg. He was one of the best known restaurateurs and hotelliers in the United States and a friend and helper to many Germans who sought his advice and aid. He took a lively part in the affairs of German organizations, like the Frohsinn, Liedertafel, Quartette Club, etc., and always devoted himself with great zeal to social and benevolent enterprises and institutions, like the German Theatre, the Volksfest and the German Protestant Orphan Asylum. He died on July 18, 1897.

knew, persuaded the duke of Orleans, regent of France, to establish a great national bank in Paris and engage in schemes to populate Louisiana, and as a part of this last undertaking he brought a shipload of German settlers, whom he placed on lands along the Mississippi River, above the city, and while the Germans had to endure many of the hardships incident to life in a new country, the German Coast of Louisiana became, under the energy, the industry and the persevering activity of these settlers, famous for its wealth and prosperity."

The story of the first German settlement in Louisiana is told at length in a book published by the late J. Hanno Deiler, professor emeritus of German in Tulane University, entitled "The Settlement of the German Coast of Louisiana and the Creoles of German Descent." From this work it appears that from 1717 to 1719 about 2,000 Germans from the Palatinate and Switzerland were sent to Louisiana by John Law, the French financial secretary. Many of them died on the voyage across the sea, of sickness caused by the privations and hardships, the miserable fare, the lack of drinking water and the terribly insanitary conditions of the vessels. The survivors settled on what is today still called "The German Coast." In 1720 more Germans arrived at New Orleans. In 1726 a colony was founded in St. Charles Parish, six miles above New Orleans, by Captain Von Ahrensburg. The hardships and undaunted perseverance of these settlers are graphically portrayed by Prof. Deiler as follows:

"No pen can describe, nor human fancy imagine, the hardships which the German pioneers of Louisiana suffered. No wonder so many of them perished. Had they been a less hardy race, not one of these families would have survived. It should be remembered that the land assigned to them was virgin forest in the heavy alluvial bottoms of the Mississippi. When the arduous work of clearing the land was done the tilling of the soil began. With plow? Oh, no! The Compagnie des Indes did not furnish plows. But why speak of plows? There were no horses nor oxen to draw them. No draught animals, no plows, no cows, no wagons to haul the products. And when the day's work in the field was done there was no evening rest inviting them home, for now began the heavy work on the pilon, the handmill or pounding trough to crush the corn and rice for their scanty meals. No meat! Where should it be obtained? The people working during the day in the fields to utter exhaustion could not go hunting for game.

"Rice, corn and beans; corn, beans and rice; beans, rice and corn constituted their daily fare, with Mississippi water to drink. One cannot blame the French engages for running away from such a miserable existence. There is in Louisiana a popular saying among Creoles when they speak of work uncommonly hard: 'It takes German people to do that.' Such is the reputation these German pioneers made for themselves in Louisiana. Yes, it took German people! They stood their work manfully, and most of them laid down and died long before their time.

"The settlers on the German Coast received re-enforcements at

JOSIAH GROSS

Mr. Gross was born at Drake, Missouri, and came to New Orleans in 1886. He is a graduate of the University of Missouri, and also graduated in law from Tulane University. He has won recognition in his calling as a lawyer and notary and also as author and student of literature and science. He is a member of the Society of American Authors and the Association for the Advancement of Science.

In 1892 Mr. Gross married Miss Caroline Zitch, a native of New Orleans.

different times.   There were many intermarriages between the German and the French and Spanish families.   In those days there was a great scarcity of women in Louisiana.   Indeed, women of the street were gathered in Paris and sent to provide wives for the colonists.   Few of these women ever had any children, and their families became extinct in the second and third generation.   No wonder that the young Frenchmen chose wives from among the German maidens, who were not only physically and morally sound and strong, but had also been reared by their German mothers to be good housewives.   Even into the most exclusive circles, into the families of the officials and of the richest merchants the German girls married.   Some became the wives of French and Spanish officers of ancient nobility.   In some of these families the German language survived for several generations, but gradually French became the family language.   German names, too, have been preserved, though usually in such mutilated forms that they can hardly be recognized.   Most of the Creoles of German descent at the present time no longer know how the names of their German ancestors looked."

Prof. Deiler concludes his book with this advice to the Creoles of German descent: "May they ever remember their German ancestors and emulate their example!"

It seems to be the universal sentiment in Louisiana today that the Germans and other nationalities from the northern part of Europe make the best settlers and citizens and are looked upon as desirable additions to our commonwealth, while immigrants from the southern part of Europe are not in demand.   That this has always been the sentiment appears from an interesting letter discovered by Prof. Deiler among copies of ancient documents in the archives of the Marine Department of France.   He made his researches at the request of the Louisiana Historical Society.   The letter is from M. Laussat, colonial prefect of Louisiana and commissioner of the French Government, and dated "New Orleans, Messidor the 8th,   in the eleventh year."   The month of Messidor began on the 19th of June and ended on the 18th of July.   The eleventh year was the year 1803.   The letter is as follows:

"The Colonial Prefect of Louisiana, to Citizen Chaptal, Minister of the Interior: Citizen Minister—I received the letter of the 4th of Floreal of this year by which your excellency deigned to consult me on the project of embarking German laborers for Louisiana.

"This is a project which should be made a regular system by the French government for several years if it wants to derive benefit from this country and to preserve it.

"Its present condition and its wretched (miserable) population demand this imperatively.   This class of peasants, and especially of that nationality, is just the class we need and the only one which always achieved perfect success in these parts.

"What is called here the 'German Coast' is the most industrious (la plus industrieuse), the most populous (la plus peuplee), the most

VALENTINE MERZ

Was born in New Albany, Ind., August 13, 1855. Came to New Orleans in 1868 and worked for his uncle, George Merz, owner of the Old Canal City Beer Brewery. For six years he was in the employ of Fellman Bros.' dry goods house. He then started on his life career of selling beer, taking over the Blatz Brewing Company's agency, and later that of the Anheuser Busch Company. In 1884 he bought out the Jules Krust Saloon, running this place for eighteen years, when he sold it to the present proprietor, C. Kolb. Mr. Mertz was then elected as president of the old New Orleans Brewing Company. Later he built the Dixie Brewing Company and was its president until prohibition forced the enterprise out of business. Mr. Merz serves on the board of directors of the Interstate Bank. He is known to be very charitable and gives quietly and often.

at ease (la plus aisee), the most upright (la plus honnete), the most respected (la plus estimee) part of the inhabitants of this colony.

"I regard it as essential that the French government should make it a rule to send every year from one thousand to twelve hundred families of the frontier departments of Switzerland, the Rhine and Holland; the emigrants of our southern provinces are not worth anything (n'y valent rien).

"LAUSSAT."

The sentiment expressed in this letter coincides exactly with the present opinion throughout the State. It is certainly true that the Germans have maintained their reputation for honesty, thrift and perseverance.

During the first half of the nineteenth century the immigration of Germans to Louisiana again assumed large proportions. New Orleans was then the gate through which the stream of immigration poured into this continent, the newcomers seeking the convenient river route to the West. Many thousands of those, however, who had planned to go up the river to the West or proceed from New Orleans to Texas, finding employment in this city, located here. During the fifties of the last century the number of German immigrants landing in New Orleans in one year, 1854, reached 40,006. The German element in this city was then at its greatest strength. It had two daily papers, a German theatre and some thirty German churches, each of which maintained a German parochial school.

Some Notable Germans of Louisiana

Among the Germans in New Orleans who acquired considerable fame during the first half of the last century were Vincenz Nolte, a banker; Christian Roselius, a noted lawyer, and Dr. Karl A. Lutzenburg. Mr. Nolte's career was full of adventures. He landed in New Orleans in 1805 at the age of 26, and fought as a volunteer under General Jackson in the battle of New Orleans, January 18, 1815. When Lafayette visited New Orleans in 1825 as a guest of honor, Nolte was a member of the reception committee, and had the honor of lending him $1,200. He was engaged in the banking business and lost his fortune in a panic in England. In 1854 he published a book in two volumes, entitled "Fifty Years in Both Hemispheres."

Roselius is well remembered as one of the greatest lawyers Louisiana has known. His fame is all the more remarkable when it is known under what difficulties he prepared himself for his profession. It has frequently been stated that Roselius was a redemptioner, as those were called who upon landing were sold to the highest bidder to work off the passage money, but this is denied by a writer in the City Directory of 1856, which also contains the fine steel engraving from which the accompanying picture is taken. As this article was written during Roselius' lifetime, it is very strong evidence. It is certain, however, that Roselius landed in New Orleans practically without means, at the

PAUL HALLER

Born May 24, 1837, in Aldingen, Wurttemberg, Germany. Came to America when a boy of 12 years, and worked as an apprentice in the tinner trade. Enlisted in the Confederate Army and served during the entire Civil War. After the war he was associated with his brother, Henry, in the tinware and house furnishing business. Was an active member of the old Mechanics, Dealers and Lumbermen's Exchange, serving as treasurer for over twenty years. He married Caroline Hesgin in 1872. He died March 26, 1897.

age of 17. He became first an apprentice to the printer's art, which occupation helped him to acquire a knowledge of good English. In 1825 Roselius commenced the first literary paper ever published in New Orleans, under the title of The Halcyon. This venture did not prove a success, as the publication was suspended after eighteen months. In the meantime Roselius had taken up the study of law, and in 1827, after a brilliant examination, he was admitted to the bar. Owing to his extensive knowledge of law he soon acquired a great reputation. In 1841 he was appointed attorney general. He was a member of the Constitutional Conventions of 1845 and 1852. He is described as a vigorous speaker. His English was so pure and correct that the most acute ear could never discover that it was not his mother tongue. He also spoke French fluently, as well as German, and had good knowledge of Latin and Spanish. As a man he was one of the kindest and most generous of his kind, so that in spite of his large income he left no large wealth. The writer above mentioned closes his sketch of Roselius with this beautiful sentence: "The pleasure of aiding those we love, of mitigating the poverty and relieving the distress of the unfortunate is worth all the pride of victory, all the power and luxury of wealth."

In this connection the names of two Germans of this period must be mentioned who became public benefactors by bequeathing their large fortunes to public benevolence. John D. Fink, who died in 1856, left an estate of over $200,000 with the direction that it be used as a fund for maintaining an asylum for widows and orphans. The Fink Asylum, on Camp and Antonine, perpetuates his memory. Kaspar Auch left his fortune of over $100,000 to the Presbyterian churches, to the end that their poor might be provided for. Mr. Auch is said to have been a redemptioner. He died in 1886.

Dr. Lutzenburg came to New Orleans with his father in 1819. Here he studied medicine and especially surgery. In 1829 he became chief surgeon of the Charity Hospital. When seized by the yellow fever, he cured himself by blood letting, which method he also pursued with his patients in spite of much opposition. He encountered similar opposition by his method of depriving smallpox patients of light to prevent disfiguring scars. A private hospital, founded by him on Elysian Fields street, bearing his name, is well remembered by older citizens. Later he became dean of the Medical College and president of several medical and scientific societies. He died in 1848.. His grandson, Chandler C. Luzenburg, is now district attorney.

Louisiana once had a governor who was a native of Germany, Michael Hahn, a pupil of Roselius, who was chief executive of the State during the first term after the Civil War. Hahnville is named after him. Governor Wiltz was a descendant of the Wiltz family, who emigrated from Thuringia, Germany, and were among the earlier settlers.

When, during the fifties of the last century, the railroads from eastern ports to the West were completed, the stream of immigration sought that shorter route, and no more Germans came to New Orleans for a while. The result has been that the German element has rapidly

EDWARD HENRY WALSDORF

Mr. Walsdorf was born in New Orleans, December 13, 1872, eldest son of the late August Walsdorf and Josephine R. Schaller. His early education was attained in the McDonogh public schools and he learned his chosen profession in the College of Pharmacy. He has been in business for himself since 1895, and at one time conducted a chain of six successful drug stores. Four years ago he established Walsdorf's Inc., Canal at Rampart Street. On September 21, 1896, he married Delia T. Stewart, of Mobile, Ala. Their three children are Edward H., Jr., Thelma Walsdorf, Richmond and Harold N. His two sons are associated with him in business.

Besides giving his time to the teaching of pharmacy at Tulane University, Mr. Walsdorf has been president of the Louisiana State Board of Pharmacy for twenty years. He also served as president of the Louisiana State Pharmaceutical Association, being elected May 13, 1913. He is a member of the Orleans Pharmaceutical Association and the New Orleans Drug Club. He is a member of the American Pharmaceutical Association, of the National Association Boards of Pharmacy, representing Louisiana, Mississippi, Florida, Alabama and Georgia, and of the National Association Boards of Pharmacy.

Mr. Walsdorf is widely known in fraternal and social organizations. In Masonry he occupies many prominent positions; he is a member of the Grand Consistory, State of Louisiana, thirty-second degree Scottish Rite, a member of the Jerusalem Temple of the Mystic Shrine, a charter member of the Order of Eastern Star, a member of Knights of Pythias, Independent Order of Odd Fellows, United Ancient Order of Druids and Loyal Order of Moose.

decreased in numbers, in proportion as the older settlers have died. The German churches are becoming more and more Americanized, the English language being now used in most of their services. But the Germans are still an important part of the body politic. In the editorial referred to, the Picayune says: "There are no people more industrious than the Germans, when serious work is to be done, but when they take recreation and diversion, they do so in real earnest and in a true spirit of innocent fun. Many of them hold positions of honor and trust. Mayor Martin Behrman is of German extraction. A. G. Ricks, commissioner of finance, and Senator Joseph Voegtle are native Germans. The German Society, of which William Frantz is president, is a body of influential men which looks back upon a history of sixty-five years. The Germans maintain two homes for the aged and infirm and two orphanages, which are all models of their kind.

In recent years German settlers have again begun to make their home in Louisiana. This was due to the efforts put forth by the State commissioner of agriculture and immigration, E. O. Bruner, and his predecessor, Charles Schuler, both of them Germans, to attract German immigration to this State.

It is said that our State has now only one-fifth of her arable land under cultivation, the other four-fifths still awaiting the spade of the agriculturist. Add to these the vast areas of land which are reclaimed by drainage and brought under the plow, bringing into the market hundreds of thousands of acres of the best farming lands. Add to this again the 1,000,000 acres of cut-over lands in this State, admirably adapted to stock raising. Who will work all this land now lying idle and producing no revenue, either to its owners or to the State? Obviously your negroes will not do it. They know nothing but cotton raising and much of this land is not suitable for that crop.

With a desirable class of immigrants these lands can be made immensely valuable. There is no other solution to the problem of developing our resources and building up the revenues of the State and strengthening its citizenship than by telling the farmers in the North and in Europe of the rare opportunities awaiting them here and inviting them to share in the blessings which a kind Providence has showered so lavishly upon this favored section of our land.

A VISIT TO THE GERMAN COLONIES IN LOUISIANA

Louisiana is one of the few States of the Union that maintains a separate bureau for the purpose of aiding immigrants, procuring positions for them if they are willing to work on the farm, or if they want to settle and engage in agricultural pursuits, giving them information and advice in regard to the selection of land suitable for their purposes. This bureau also sees that the immigrants do not fall into the hands of selfish and designing men. But this bureau does more— it keeps an eye upon the people even after they have located; it gives

PETER JUNG, SR.

Born in New Orleans, 1858. Started in the furniture business, at Ninth and Tchoupitoulas Streets. Started iron bed business in 1900. Is president of the Crescent Bed Company and proprietor of the Jung Hotel.

them advice and information concerning our methods of agriculture, shipping facilities, and hundreds of other things which immigrants have to learn; it endeavors to protect them in their right, if necessary.

Prior to the World War, which put a stop to all German immigration, the Louisiana State Bureau of Agriculture and Immigration conducted a vigorous campaign to secure German settlers. As the writer planned a trip to Europe in the summer of 1906, he was asked by Col. Chas. Schuler, Commissioner of Agriculture and Immigration, to invite German immigrants to our State. I promised to do all I could. Armed with a commission from Governor Blanchard, I interviewed newspaper editors in all the large cities of Germany and Switzerland, offering them articles setting forth the advantages of Louisiana. These editors showed little desire to promote immigration to the United States, expressing it as their opinion that Germans coming to America are easily assimilated to the new country and lost to their native land. Out of four newspapers in Berlin interviewed, only one agreed to publish such an article. This was the "Echo," a periodical for Germans in foreign lands. The effect of this article was remarkable. Letters of inquiry soon arrived from Germany, Austria, Hungary, Spain, Sweden, Russia, Mexico, Guatemala, Canada, Palestine, the Straits Settlements, the Samoa Islands, South America and Africa. The writer was then requested to act as German correspondent for the Bureau of Immigration. As such he not only answered all German letters, but also prepared a pamphlet of 54 pages, entitled "Louisiana's Invitation to German Farmers and Colonists." This booklet was afterwards translated into the Dutch, French, Italian, Ruthenian, Polish, Croatian and Slavonian languages. He also continued regularly to publish articles in the Echo. As a result of this propaganda, many Germans settled in Louisiana. To look into the welfare of the newly arrived as well as most of the older settlers, the Commissioner of Immigration sent his secretary, Mr. J. L. Knoepfler, and the writer on tours of inspection to visit all the German colonies throughout the State of Louisiana.

The first trip embraced the rice country around Crowley. Mr. W. W. Duson, a noted citizen of the latter place, expressed it as his decided opinion that the Germans had been the most successful settlers in the rice section, and almost without exception they arrived without means, but by their accustomed industry, they soon acquired property, and most of them a fortune. He remarked that Germans who have not succeeded in and around Crowley are so rare that you would have to look for them with a lantern.

However, we were not satisfied with this testimony from the lips of a third, no matter however reliable the witness, but went to hear from the mouths of the German settlers themselves how they had begun, and how they had succeeded. We visited the members of the large German Colony at St. Leo, four miles from Rayne, which is exclusively German. Mr. Jos. Heinen, one of the patriarchs of this colony, arrived here in 1882, and he now owns 2,200 acres of land

FRANCIS RICKERT

Mr. Rickert was born in Holstein, Germany, in 1820, emigrated to this country in 1841 and landed in New York. After two years he moved to New Orleans, where he entered the mercantile business and later became the vice president and manager of the Teutonia Insurance Company. This office he filled until his death, in 1889. He was president of the German Society from 1873 until his death. He was one of the organizers of the German Protestant Orphan Asylum and a member of its board and the board of the Fink Asylum. He took active interest in all progressive enterprises in the city. His grandsons, Frank M. and Frederick W. Rickert, own and successfully operate one of the largest and most modern rice mills in the South.

worth $100,000. He had six married children, all living in comfortable circumstances. Out of his thirty grandchildren he had only lost three by death. This proves that the climate is conducive to health. We asked him if they had ever suffered from rice fever, and he replied that this fever was unknown there.

Mr. Nicholas J. Zaunbrecher, another patriarch of St. Leo, like Mr. Heinen, came from the Rhine Province, and now owns a large estate. He was very conservative in his opinion as to the chances of success for German settlers at this time. At the present price of land they must expect to meet considerable difficulties in the beginning, but if rice maintained its present price, and the newcomers secured good land, they could still make money.

Mr. J. R. Schoen, a recent arrival, having only come here in December, 1907, from Indiana, proved that settlers can still succeed in this section. He bought forty acres of land and made $800 from his first rice crop. This year he rented ninety-five acres for rice and used his own land for feed crop. He had never had to pay one cent for doctors' bills since his arrival, and stated that neither he nor his family had ever expressed the desire to return to Indiana.

Similar reports were received from other colonists. We will cite a few of those who came to Louisiana through reading the "Echo."

Mr. A. Schaer came from the Transvaal, in South Africa. He had tried for a number of years to make a success in Africa by raising stock. He located in North Louisiana.

Mr. and Mrs. C. Hoffman also came from the Transvaal. Mr. Hoffman had been a civil engineer, receiving a salary of $187 per month. He gave up this lucrative position to engage in argicultural pursuits in Louisiana. Upon his arrival here, he at first worked in the American Sugar Refinery at a good salary. Col. Chas. Schuler, Commissioner of Agriculture, offered him the free use of a number of acres on his own plantation in De Soto Parish for three years. Mr. Hoffman accepted the proposition. He began at once to plant corn, cotton, truck, etc.; bought two mules, several hogs, and also a country store. He bought another forty acres from Col. Schuler, which he rented out. Mr. Hoffman thought that Northern Louisiana is well adapted for a German Colony, but at least twenty families would have to be settled in one locality, and at least one among them must be familiar with the English language and our local conditions. He has been instrumental in bringing two other German families to Louisiana.

Mr. and Mrs. Konrad Klinghardt arrived from Germany. He was only 22 years of age, and had pursued the study of law in Germany, but upon the advice of his physician decided to engage in agricultural pursuits. He located in Rapides Parish, near Alexandria. Although having had no experience in this line, by commendable zeal and diligence, he succeeded. From a single acre planted in potatoes, after the German fashion of using plenty of stable manure, they obtained 180 bushels, which brought $149.00, and seed enough for their fall crop. Mr. Klinghardt became a member of the German Society in 1917.

GEORGE WILLIAM RUEFF

Was born at Sultz, Germany, on November 10, 1838, and died in New Orleans on December 5, 1924. Mr. Rueff came to New Orleans at the age of 16, and engaged in the customhouse brokerage business. He was the founder and up to the date of his death the president and directing head of "George William Rueff, Inc.," the oldest customhouse brokerage firm in the city.

Mr. Rueff was prominent in fraternal, social and civic activities and was a Royal Arch Mason. He was an active member of the German Society, the German Protestant Orphans' Home and many other charitable institutions.

Mr. Hy. Rohrs came from Idaho and located in Alexandria. He commenced by renting 20 acres of land and a residence and raising truck for the market in Alexandria. He was well satisfied with the good results of his labor.

Mr. G. O. Heinrich and wife arrived from Germany. Mr. Heinrich had previously been engaged on a cocoa plantation in German East Africa. After working for a season on shares near Clinton, he bought 100 acres and went into the stock raising business.

Mr. August Wittmer arrived here from Chicago, where he had been located for 16 years. He located at Raceland, and is well satisfied. He has a family of ten healthy children.

Both the German and Belgian Colonies are noted for the number of children in each family. Eight is the average number per family, but often ten and twelve are found. Race suicide cannot be held against them.

We then visited some of the older German settlements at Shreveport, Bayou Sara, St. Francisville and Clinton. We gave them information as to shipping facilities, better methods for diversified farming, etc. Although some of these Germans are located 12 miles from the railroad, they have nevertheless succeeded and have accumulated money.

In visiting the colonists we did not fail also to visit the prominent citizens and land holders in every community. We thoroughly discussed the question of immigration with them, and took a memorandum of the lands which they offer.

_____

The German Society expresses its hearty appreciation of the efforts made by the Louisiana Bureau of Agriculture and Immigration in past years to attract desirable settlers to our State, and indulges in the hope that in the not distant future similar efforts may be resumed. The reasons why the State of Louisiana is in need of immigration are manifold. Vast areas of land may yet be reclaimed and brought under the plow. Who will settle on them? Obviously, with the boll weevil active, it will not be wise to introduce the culture of cotton there. Truck farming is the other alternative.

The diversification of crops involves more constant and individual attention on the part of the farmer than has been the case among the cotton planters. We must have farmers who are willing to go into the field themselves and do their own work without depending upon negroes. We will have to look to other countries than ours for this desirable type of citizen. That is the chief reason why Louisiana needs immigrants. Our planters up to now have planted cotton and depended for their supplies upon the West. We must have farmers who will produce everything they need and buy nothing.

_____

"TWO SPLENDID GERMANS IN LOUISIANA"

The Illinois Staats Zeitung, of Chicago, on Sept. 25, 1926, says under the caption, "Two Splendid Men From Germany in Louisiana":

Mr. Charles Schuler, the able and efficient German Commissioner of

Agriculture and Immigration of the State of Louisiana, residing at the Capital of Baton Rouge, has honored us with a visit. He hails from the town of Maehringen, in the Black Forest, District of Horb, Kingdom of Wurttemberg. He left his home when a mere boy and came to Louisiana, where he became a farmer. In this pursuit he worked himself up by means of his steady qualities and acquired such a high standing that several years ago he was not only intrusted with the important office of Commissioner of Agriculture, a position which corresponds in the German States with the high office of Minister of Agriculture, but was also made Commissioner of Immigration. This we have not learned from his own lips, but from his distinguished countryman, the German professor, Johann Hanno Deiler, of New Orleans, who has earned great fame by his historical researches relating to the German element of Louisiana, as President of the German Society of Louisiana and likewise as President of the North American Saenger-Bund. Schuler presents to this day a splendid type of German manhood.

During next year he proposes for the first time since his emigration to visit the Fatherland, in company with Prof. Deiler. Both will then exert themselves to spread correct knowledge concerning the State of Louisiana among the people of the Fatherland. As to this State, that is making great strides to shake off the old drowsiness that prevailed in the South in the days of slavery, Pastor Voss, of New Orleans, writes in an essay, published with the approval of both these gentlemen, as follows:

"Whoever can secure a livelihood in the old country should not emigrate, but many are forced by necessity or unfavorable conditions to leave the Fatherland. To such people who wish or may be forced to find a new home in another hemisphere, and cast their eyes in the direction of the United States of America, the State of Louisiana may be a welcome haven. There is in that State still an abundance of fertile land, located in a high and healthy altitude, to be had at very low prices; and since in addition to its railroads this State also possesses innumerable waterways, on which the crops can be cheaply and readily shipped to the markets, and the farmer is able on account of the mild climate to work all the year round in the open air, harvesting two or three crops, while cattle and horses fatten on the pastures for at least ten months, requiring but two months of dry feeding, the settler may secure for himself in a few years an independent future and a highly comfortable existence. True, the colonists must have some means in order to pay the first installment on the lands they wish to acquire, as well as to secure the costs of the first seeding, the establishment of fences and the construction of the necessary dwellings and outhouses, until they can harvest the first crop. This requires a sum of about 2,000 marks. But if a man is without any means he can nevertheless secure for himself a good living, because the large plantation owners will cheerfully place at the disposal of a German settler a sufficient parcel of land, together with the tools of husbandry, horses and wagon, upon condition that one-half of the crops shall go to the owner."

HISTORY OF THE GERMAN SOCIETY

The Beginnings of the German Society

The German Society of New Orleans was organized originally solely for the relief of the thousands of German immigrants who during the forties and fifties of the last century landed in sailing vessels, many of them destitute and in a deplorable condition. New Orleans was then the chief gate of entrance through which the stream of immigrants poured into this country, because before the building of the railroads from the Atlantic coast to the West, the Mississippi River formed the most convenient route for the thousands whose destination was the Western States or Texas. Many, however, finding employment here, and perhaps lacking the means to continue their journey up the river, located in this city. Their descendants to the third and fourth generation form a large part of our population today.

According to the census of 1850, the population of New Orleans in that year was 119,460, with 11,425 Germans, not including their children born here. In 1860 the population of the city is given as 174,491, with 19,553 Germans born in Germany.

The number of German immigrants landing in New Orleans in 1850 is given roughly as 13,000, in 1851 as 25,000, in 1852 as 32,000, in 1853 as 36,000, and the peak of German immigration was reached in 1854, when 40,006 German immigrants stepped on shore in New Orleans. From that time on there was a steady decrease. In 1860 7,535 Germans landed here. With the outbreak of the Civil War, in 1861, immigration naturally ceased altogether, except for the few who came here from other parts of the country. And since the Civil War the number of newcomers through this port has been insignificant, though foreigners still continued to come to this country in large numbers. Immigration reached its highest level in 1882, when 684,186 immigrants came to the United States, including 250,630 Germans. New York had become the almost exclusive port of debarcation, because all the steamship lines from Europe had that port as their destination. Swift steamships had begun to replace the slow sailing vessels, especially the numerous smaller ones, and the building of the transcontinental railways afforded a quick journey to the West. Only a few stragglers came to New Orleans. Under our present laws restricting immigration, the number of Germans arriving at New Orleans is very limited, notwithstanding the building of a fine Immigration Station below our city, by the U. S. government.

From the figures given above, it will be seen that at the time of the organization of the German Society there existed already a strong German colony in New Orleans of not less than 10,000 persons born in Germany. There were thirteen German churches and numerous other

German organizations. Deiler enumerates four Catholic and nine Protestant German churches organized before 1847.* A German news paper, the Courier, was founded by Jos. Cohn in 1842. In its second issue this paper published an appeal to form a German society for the relief of the shipwrecked passengers of the ship Oceana, which had foundered with 241 passengers, mostly German, a month before, near Jamaica. The passengers had been brought to New Orleans. At a meeting held in the engine house, No. 4 Old Levee (now South Peters) Street, $817 was collected. Old clothes were also provided and a committee of German physicians appointed to treat passengers who had been removed to the Charity Hospital sick of fever. Some of the passengers were sent to the West, their original destination. This society then disbanded. But when the number of new arrivals increased from year to year, many of them destitute, a permanent organization to aid and assist them seemed imperative. A writer in the Courier pointed to the fact that the failure of crops in Germany and a severe winter would result in a larger immigration, especially of the poorer classes, and steps should be taken at once to aid them upon their arrival. In the next issue of the Courier the German public was requested to attend a meeting at the Conti Street Hotel, on Conti, between Old Levee and Chartres Streets, on May 5, 1847, at 7:30 p. m., for the purpose of organizing a German Society for New Orleans, like that of New York, which had already existed for 20 years.

The meeting was held. Christian Roselius, a noted German lawyer, presided. A resolution was adopted to form such a society as soon as 150 members and $2,000 in voluntary subscriptions had been secured. Within two weeks the committee reported 397 members and $3,075 in gifts, and on May 24 a temporary constitution of the German Society of New Orleans was adopted. The Germans in Lafayette, now a suburb of New Orleans, joined the new organization. Even the consuls of the old country eagerly supported a movement which promised to relieve them of the care for the immigrants, and two of them became the first officers of the society. Wm. Vogel, Consul of Prussia, Hamburg and Oldenburg, was elected its first president, at a meeting held June 2, 1847; J. H. Eimer. Consul of Austria and Baden, first vice-president; Dr. E. Authenried, second vice-president; J. D. Kamper, treasurer; J. F. Behnker, recording secretary; A. Schneider, financial secretary, with the following as directors: Geo. Dirmeyer, F. W. Freudenthal, Consul of Nassau; L. A. Gunst, P. William, M. Schneider, V. von Voigts, Dr. D. S. Gans, F. Honold, Consul of Wurttemberg; P. E. Hunten, H. G. Schmidt, C. A. Fidler, J. Schuhmann.

A permanent constitution was adopted, an office rented in St. Louis Street and J. U. Haussner was engaged as agent and collector at an annual salary of $900. A circular was printed in 1,000 copies and sent to ship agents, captains, to European ports and to all others interested,

---

*The total number of German churches organized in New Orleans and its suburbs up to the year 1881 is 7 Catholic and 32 Protestant churches. Many of these are now extinct. In 1886 there were in New Orleans 7 German Catholic parochial schools with 1,831 pupils, and 15 Protestant with 1,174 pupils.

acquainting them with the purposes of the society, and so, on July 1, 1847, began the business activity of the German Society of New Orleans.

_____

Hardships of the Immigrants

The hardships of immigrants in those days were great and the sufferings of most of them intense. The journey on the sailing vessels lasted from 70 to 120 days. The provisions for the comfort and well-being of the passengers were of the most primitive kind and utterly inadequate. There was insufficient ventilation, sanitation was totally neglected and the food was bad or insufficient. Even drinking water was not supplied in sufficient quantity. The Liverpool vessel America, with 493 passengers, had only one cooking hearth, 5 by 3 feet in dimension, for all these people, so that each family could cook its meals only once in four days. There were no separate hospital facilities for the sick. Sometimes dangerous diseases spread among the passengers and hundreds died on the way and were buried at sea. On a ship coming from Bremen 80 persons out of 500 passengers died of a disease similar to cholera. The ship landed at a small island and was disinfected with lime, which checked the disease. Already during its first business year the society picked up 30 children whose parents had died on the sea, and placed them in institutions or good private families. Their names were entered in a book with a statement of the articles from the effects of the deceased parents which had been taken charge of by kind fellow-passengers or ship captains for these children and were turned over to the society, such as a Bible, a pair of spectacles, an attestation of conduct, prayer books, rings, passports, etc. Many of these children were formally adopted and received other names.

Prof. Deiler relates the case of a well known dentist who had been adopted by a highly respectable Creole family and who was identified by a prayer book found after the death of his benefactor, which contained the names of his parents, who had died on the sea, with the date of their marriage. Thus he learned his original German name and also discovered a brother and sister, believed dead for forty years, but living all these years in the city without suspecting the nearness of the brother.

The first German orphanage, the Catholic St. Joseph's Orphan Asylum, was founded in 1853, the German Protestant Orphan Asylum and the Lutheran Bethlehem Orphanage in 1866. (See Deiler's History of German Churches in Louisiana.)

But the hardships on the sea were not the only ones which the immigrants encountered. Their inexperience and helplessness were often taken advantage of by unscrupulous people. Even steamship agents and ship captains were guilty of exploiting these plain and unsophisticated travelers. In one instance, a sailing vessel dumped its passengers, with their luggage, on shore at the mouth of the river, 107 miles from New Orleans, depriving them of the usual privilege of remaining on board two or three days after their arrival and putting them to great trouble and expense in moving their baggage to the city. It must be remembered that these immigrants usually brought with them all their household effects in wooden boxes, the size of which was sometimes that of a small one-story house. These had sometimes been damaged by handling on the journey and when they were hoisted from the ship, half of the contents would be spilled on deck or fall back into the ship's hold. In 1853 the ship Reform, destined for Galveston, foundered near Nuevitas. Its 94 passengers, deprived of all their belongings, reached Havana, whence they were sent by the German Aid Society of that city to New Orleans. The German Society helped them to proceed on their way to Texas.

Sometimes immigrants were persuaded by agents in European ports to travel by way of New Orleans, on the plea that from there they could get passage to any desired point. Some had been told that from here they could easily reach La Guayra, in Venezuela; others that they could get weekly accommodation to Montevideo. Of course, no ships sailed from New Orleans to those distant ports, and the poor dupes were left stranded thousands of miles from their destination.

Others were cheated by ticket agents, who sold them bogus tickets to inland points. In Havre such swindlers charged immigrants double fare for the trip from New Orleans to St. Louis, but accepted one-half of it as "payment on account," with a certificate entitling the holder to a quick passage on a Mississippi steamer. The German Society requested European governments to place all passenger agents under bond.

But the troubles of immigrants, which began before they started their sea voyage and multiplied on the ocean, did not end there. When they landed, they were beset by agents and runners in the interest of boarding house keepers and Mississippi steamers. Often these fellows would seize the baggage of the immigrants and carry it away, compelling them to follow. They received a head tax of 50 cents for every passenger or boarder secured. Some of these man hunters established themselves at the mouth of the river and, boarding an immigrant vessel, plied their trade with smooth tongue among the passengers. The German Society issued 3,000 circulars, warning passengers against these nefarious people and urged them to await the agents of the Society upon landing. Captains of reliable river boats were requested to land their vessels alongside of the immigrant ships and to receive the baggage of the passengers directly on their boats after it had passed inspection by the customs officers, and so break up the business of these runners.

The majority of the immigrants were people of moderate means. Many were destitute. European communities would ship their undesirables to this country to get rid of them. In 1852 one hundred poverty-stricken people landed who had been sent by communities in Baden. They had received three gulden ($1.20) each as spending money. Other communities, mostly Swiss, had shipped undesirables in a similar manner, but provided them more liberally with 25 gulden for the inland trip. The report of the German Society for the year 1854-5 states that with few exceptions the immigrants of that year were people of sufficient means to pay for their own support in the beginning until they secured a foothold, people therefore whom this country should welcome. Among the exceptions were 133 poverty-stricken people who had been expelled by their home town guaranteeing their passage money and threatening them that unless they emigrated to America they would receive no more assistance at home. They had been told the German Society would take care of them. Among the number were crippled and infirm persons, unmarried and widowed women, and 42 minor children. They were landed in the Third Municipality (now the Third District) and when expelled from there, were transferred or smuggled to the upper city. The report of the German Society states:

"At the sight of the intense misery of these unfortunates, many of them almost naked and all of them destitute and without shelter against the bitter cold (they had left home in December), we determined to provide and care for them."

But such cases were exceptional. State Secretary A. A. Upshur says in his report to the President of the United States, November 24, 1843:

"We receive from the States associated in the German Union most valuable immigrants, consisting chiefly of farmers of excellent character and industrious habit, who bring to their adopted country sufficient gold and silver to enable them to purchase and settle lands."— (President's Message, I. Session, 28th Congress.)

The same official reports:

"From 1835 to 1839 emigration from Bavaria to America alone was 18,931, who, according to Bavarian government reports, carried with them nearly seven millions of gulden in spite of the heavy tax on all things taken out of the country."

Hon. G. C. Verplanck, President of the Commissioners of Immigration, New York, reports on January 23, 1857, to the State Department:

"There is a marked contrast in passengers coming by the way of Hamburg and Bremen and those by other European ports. It rarely occurs that passengers from either Hamburg or Bremen are unable, on their arrival here, to pay their way to their destination in the interior, or to secure all proper comforts and conveniences on the way."—Senate Documents, I. Session, 35th Congress.

Revolutionists of 1848

During the early fifties of the last century many German revolutionists sought refuge on our shores. They belonged to the most intelligent and best educated class of people—officials, scientists, artists, students, young and old, who had learned everything except that which was essential to success in this country—to work. Raised in monarchi-

al countries and sorely disappointed at the result of the revolution of
848 and 1849, which they had supported with all the ardor of their
ieart, deprived of their positions and prospects of such, compelled to
lee their countries as exiles and facing a struggle for existence, for
vhich they were unprepared by previous training and experience, these
)eople brought peculiar ideas and ideals with them.   They considered
hemselves superior to all the others and demanded of the Germans in
:he South that under their leadership an organization should be formed
it once to suppress slavery in the Southern States.   As this could not
be done, and as it did not conflict with their ideas of liberty to denounce
everybody who dared to differ with them, the result was a break, a
conflict between the "greenhorns" and the "graybeards," which lasted
until the greenhorns, too, had turned gray and had recognized by
experience the impracticability of their extreme ideas.   From that
time on, leadership among the Germans was willingly accorded them
and subsequently many of them were called to responsible and honorable positions.   New Orleans also received its quota of revolutionists
and there were not lacking unpleasant controversies.   They came without means, confidently expecting to be received here with open arms
and to find here a safe and carefree refuge.   However, they soon
discovered that in this country, with all its liberty, they had no other
choice than to look for work without loss of time or to starve.   As
they were unqualified for hard labor, it was extremely difficult for
them· to find a suitable position corresponding with their wishes and
abilities, and but few of them were ready to assume a subordinate
position.

The Tragedy of the Yellow Fever Scourge

A large part of the work of the German Society during the first
half of its life consisted in ministering to the yellow fever victims
during the epidemics which periodically afflicted our city in those years,
resulting in the death of thousands, especially among the unacclimated
foreigners, and in incalculable damage to the city's commerce by the
quarantines raised on every side.   Happily, our city has been perma-
nently delivered from this scourge.   A generation has grown up that
has never seen a case of yellow fever.   The discovery, not of the
cause of the disease, but of the way in which it is transmitted from
sick to sound persons, made an intelligent and effective warfare against
it possible.   Before that time men were fighting in the dark and only
wasting their energies.   Many a person was afraid to breathe, thinking
the fever germs were "in the air" and that he might inadvertently in-
hale them.   Or he was afraid to ride in the street cars or mingle
among people, lest he should catch the disease from his neighbor.   The
German Society warned the newcomers against drinking too much water
or eating fresh fruit.   All such fears have been shown to be ground-
less, since it was discovered early in this century that yellow fever,
like malaria, is propagated only by a certain species of the mosquito,

which sucks the fever microbes from a sick person and by stinging transmits them into the blood of a healthy person. This theory explains the otherwise inexplicable fact why yellow fever is killed by the first frost—it is because the frost kills the mosquitoes.

Prior to 1853 New Orleans had been exempt from a yellow fever scourge for a few years. Already it was hoped that on account of the clearing of the woods and draining of the swamp between the city and the lake, New Orleans would not be afflicted any more by the fever, when in 1853 the city was visited by the worst epidemic in its history, with 8,000 deaths caused by it alone. The report of the German Society of that year estimates the number of Germans who succumbed to it as 5,500. When it is remembered that in that year 24,270 German immigrants landed in New Orleans, it will be seen that the Society was hard pressed to relieve the distress among the new arrivals. The most important task was to remove newcomers as quickly as possible up the Mississippi River. The newly formed "Howard Association" looked after the sick in the city. Temporary hospitals and orphanages were erected, free markets were opened, all possible measures were taken to stop the spread of the yellow pest—it was all in vain. People dropped dead in the streets. In houses visited by the relief corps they found half-famished children lying on the corpses of their parents. Whole families were extinguished. Surviving children, especially those too young to know their family names, were forever separated. They may have lived near each other without ever knowing one another as brothers or sisters.

The German Society, whose members were sorely tried in their own families, worked in conjunction with the Howard Association in doing what was possible with the steadily decreasing number of its own members. Under the direction of its agent, J. B. Schroeder, it erected four branch offices, with the sub agents, C. F. Wagner, at the corner of Delord and Carondelet streets; Carl Nathan, at 42 Toulouse street; August Hoppe, at Moreau and Enghien streets, and F. Benter, at Tchoupitoulas and Philip streets, whose duty it was to visit the sick Germans, report them to the Howard Asociation, remove them to hospitals and to act as interpreters. But each of them had many more cases than he could possibly attend. The sick remonstrated against being taken to the hospital. Private physicians were so overtaxed that they declined help. Many patients died without attention. Finally the agents themselves took sick. Others took their places until these in turn were stricken. The misery was beyond all description. At the annual meeting of the German Society in September, usually attended by 200, only four members appeared. The number of orphans turned over to the Society during this year was surprisingly small, only six. "The children followed their parents into the grave, if they had not preceded them."

On October 19 of that year, when the fever still claimed many victims every day, the German bark Dorette appeared without previous announcement at the mouth of the Mississippi River with 313 German immigrants. As the city did nothing, the German Society secured an order from the military governor to detain the vessel until the Society could send a well provisioned steamer to receive the passengers and, passing the city under full steam, bring them to St. Louis, where they all landed safe and sound.

What the German Society Did for the Immigrants

The main work of the Society during the first forty years of its activities consisted in aiding the immigrants upon landing, not only at the customs inspection, but in all other matters, assisting those bound for the North and West to continue on their journey up the Mississippi River, and in finding employment for those who intended to make their home in New Orleans or Louisiana. The majority of the immigrants landing here took advantage of the services rendered by the agents of the Society free of charge. Needy immigrants received free transportation through the Society and provisions for the rest of the trip. As has already been shown, the Society took measures to remedy abuses in the treatment of passengers on sailing vessels and river steamers, as also in boarding houses. In several instances the Society entered suit in behalf of injured passengers against delinquent parties. Orphans whose parents had died on the way or since their arrival were placed in homes or asylums. Thousands found employment through the efforts of its agents.

Securing employment for laborers and female servants was a comparatively easy matter, as the demand for this kind of labor was great. The building of several railroads, like the present Illinois Central and Southern Pacific lines, gave employment to thousands. The planters were also eager to secure German laborers. A Mr. Carroll offered to take 25 German families, build a house for each and assign sufficient land for their own support, if they would agree to work for him in planting and harvesting his crops at high wages. But owners of large plantations were not willing to sell any part of their land to settlers, even after the Civil War. They only wanted "hands" to take the place of the liberated slaves, who had left the plantations in large numbers. The German Society never encouraged this, but even warned against such efforts to secure white laborers in place of the negroes. Nevertheless, plantation life seemed to have a peculiar attraction to some Germans and many thousands accepted work there at a dollar or less per day, with free board and lodging.

Female servants were always in great demand. At one time the large supply caused a slump in the wages offered. In later years German girls preferred work in factories and shops to domestic service. During the hard times of the last decade of the last century many people tried to do without foreign help.

The Society, as a rule, received but little thanks from those who had received its benevolences; to the contrary, it was often criticized. Even the crowding of the river steamers was laid at its door. How

could such overcrowding be prevented, when it is remembered that
sometimes on the same day which brought five vessels with German
immigrants to this port, English vessels with Irish passengers also
arrived, all eager to continue their journey on the same day. In times
of cholera and yellow fever it was essential to move passengers without
delay, to place them beyond infection. If some of these, carrying the
germs of the disease in them, were taken sick and died on the way,
who could be blamed for it?

But cases of gratitude were not lacking. In one instance three
men refunded with their thanks the amounts they had received from
the Society in former years. The government of Baden sent the Society
$200 "as partial payment for the assistance given to destitute immi-
grants from the town of Neuenkirchen," and the Canton of Aargau, in
Switzerland, sent $13.50 once and later $37 more.

The annual reports of the Society for the first forty years contain
careful statistics of all cases handled, without giving the totals, except
that of the number of Germans who landed in New Orleans from June
1, 1847, to May 1, 1887, which is given as 284,918. This agrees approx-
imately with the totals the writer obtained by adding the figures for
each of the forty years. He also obtained the following totals by a
similar addition:

Persons aided in reaching St. Louis, 118,094.

Persons aided in reaching destinations on the Ohio river, 39,372.

Persons aided in reaching Texas, 21,838.

Persons for whom employment was secured, 72,690.

The total given in cash to needy applicants during the first fifty
years amounted to $17,500.00.

These are staggering figures. No pen can describe what heroic
service, what infinite patience they involve, in the face of unreason-
able demands made upon the Society at times, and unjust complaints
against it.

A Change of Policy

We have seen how the stream of immigrants pouring into this country was diverted from this port and the number of newcomers by way
of New Orleans gradually dwindled down to almost nothing. In 1871-72,
491 German immigrants passed through here and proceeded up the
river. In 1875-76 their number fell to—two persons! Under these
circumstances, the activities of the German Society were limited to
those of an Employment Bureau—finding work for those already here.
This great work, of which the general public heard but seldom, resulted in a belief that there was nothing more to do for the Society
and no more need for such an organization. The question was asked:
"Why a German Society? What is it doing? What becomes of the
membership dues? Why maintain an office and even a reserve fund?"
The membership of the Society steadily diminished, until it reached
its lowest ebb in 1879, when it had only 74 members. Manifestly, the

German Society had served its original purpose—that of ministering to immigrants—but now there was but little need of that.

There had been for some time a strong party within the Society who were of the opinion that its activities should not be restricted to newly arrived immigrants, but embrace also Germans living in New Orleans. They were, however, opposed by a few ultra-conservative leaders who believed that things should remain as they had been from the beginning. The carrying out of the idea of the progressive members had been obstructed by the provision in the constitution of the Society which required the keeping intact of a fund of $15,000 and a reserve fund of $1,500, and allowing only the interest of these funds to be used. Finally, in 1860, it was agreed to raise a special reserve fund in addition to the other, for the purpose of erecting an asylum or home for convalescent Germans, discharged from hospitals, but unable to earn a living, until their complete recovery. This special fund in a short time reached the sum of $6,000. A square of ground, bounded by Bienville, Customhouse, White and Dupre streets, was purchased for $3,418. This caused great enthusiasm among the Germans of New Orleans. The members of the German Society increased to 200. The proceeds of a Volksfest added $2,000 to the fund. Then came the Civil War, and the building of the asylum was postponed. Nevertheless, the fund increased to $12,680. Through the failure, on account of the war, of a firm in which part of the money had been invested, the fund lost $5,322. A little house was erected on the ground, at a cost of $1,359, and the place was rented to a gardener, but as the place was subject to constant overflow, it was hard to collect the rent and the revenue derived from it was small. The ground depreciated in value, and in 1867 it was sold to the City Railroad Company for $3,000. A motion to donate this fund to the German Protestant Orphan Asylum was defeated and the fund was added to the general fund of the Society, to be used to attract German immigrants to Louisiana. In the place of the Asylum Committee, a Committee on Immigration was appointed. This committee urged the erection of an immigration station in New Orleans and because it was realized that the funds of the Society were not sufficient to establish and maintain such a station with all the necessary equipment, an appeal was made to the State Legislature to appropriate $20,000 for this purpose. The measure was adopted by the House of Representatives, but defeated in the Senate. Thereupon the matter of immigration was dropped for a time.

New Activities

In 1889, Prof. J. Hanno Deiler, who had become a member of the German Society in 1879, proposed the creation of an Archive and Library Committee to gather material bearing on the history of the Germans on the Lower Mississippi. His suggestion was adopted, though not without "shaking of the head" by some of the conservative directors. This committee, in the course of years, gathered a library of many hundreds of books and pamphlets, all carefully listed in its annual reports to the Society. In the new quarters of the Society these will again be arranged on convenient shelves, easy of access to any persons interested.

In 1890 the investments of the Society amounted to $19,485. Vice President Otto Knoop moved that a donation of $1,000 be given to the German Protestant Home for the Aged and Infirm, which had been organized in 1885. As there was some objection to this, on the ground that the increase of the capital was due to the enhanced market value of the investments, which might be reduced again, Prof. Deiler moved to donate $250 to the Home for this year, on the ground that in former years the Society had collected funds for the erection of an Asylum for Convalescent Germans, but had not been able to carry out its plans. This motion was adopted. In subsequent years similar donations brought the aggregate given to the Home for the Aged by the Society to $1,200.

In 1892 it was resolved to donate monthly $10 to Parker's Convalescent Home, on Claiborne street. This aid was continued for several years, and that institution received a total of $540 from the Society up to 1897.

In the same year a committee was appointed for the enlargement of the purposes and aims of the Society and a corresponding change of the Constitution and By-Laws. According to the constitution adopted in 1874, the purpose of the Society was to assist German immigrants, while the charter of 1872 said: "To give advice and assistance to German immigrants and other Germans coming to or residing in this city." The constitution also provided that financial assistance should be given only to German immigrants, while the charter made no such restriction.

In 1894, Prof. Deiler proposed the appointing of a committee to induce German immigrants to settle in Louisiana and to encourage German steamship lines to run their ships directly to New Orleans. This caused a heated controversy in the Board of Directors, President Brandner and Vice President Knoop making strenuous objections to the plan as being outside of the purposes of the German Society, but at a general meeting of all the members the proposed measures carried with only the above two negative votes. President Brandner then resigned and Wm. Frantz was elected in his place. The charter was amended by the addition to the article defining the purposes of the Society, of the words "to attract German immigrants," which was adopted by the unanimous vote of all members except that of President Brandner.

President Deiler's Administration

During the following year Prof. Deiler was elected president. The first and most important thing done under his administration was the publication by the Society of the book written by himself, entitled,

"Louisiana, a Home for German Settlers," in 10,000 copies. The expense of publication was only $520. The Young Men's Business League had certain parts of the book, viz., the chapters dealing with the climate and health conditions of Louisiana, translated into English in 100,000 copies, scattered in all parts of the United States and England. As a result of this book, numerous inquiries about our State were received.

It was a victory for Deiler's ideas and the beginning of a new era in German immigration to Louisiana. It led to the vigorous campaign inaugurated in its behalf by the State Commissioner of Agriculture and Immigration and its results described in a previous chapter. Mr. Knoepfler, Secretary to the Commissioner of Immigration, appeared before the Board of Directors, at their request, to report about the European trip of the Commissioner, Col. Schuler, and his secretary. It was learned on this occasion that the German government forbids the emigration of unmarried women unless some responsible party at the port of landing vouches for their being placed in respectable families. The United States Government allows them to land only under the same condition. As German servant girls are in great demand here, the Board of Directors caused a declaration to that effect to be transmitted to the German and the United States Governments.

In his last annual report to the Society, written a few months before his death, President Deiler says:

"During the past year the State of Louisiana received four German families, now located in Ponchatoula, three in Alexandria, and one in Keatchie. Besides these there came to the State, through the efforts of the State Immigration Board, twenty-two German families from Pittsburg, now located in Monroe, Girard, Waterproof, St. Joseph, Hamburg and Arnaudville, La. Besides these, about thirty other families came here from other States, concerning whom the State Immigration Bureau has promised a report as soon as a trip of inspection is completed, which is now being made by the secretary, J. L. Knoepfler, and Rev. Louis Voss. The latter has been writing up the State in German newspapers, and in reply to his articles letters of inquiry have been received from every part of the world. It is with a view to gathering material for other articles that these gentlemen are now visiting the various German settlements throughout the State."

And he asks this question: "What would the United States be today if, during the past century, twenty million European immigrants had not landed here, and what would become of the United States, with its tendency to acquire wealth without labor, if those should succeed who would entirely suppress immigration?"

A Tribute to Prof. J. Hanno Deiler

In his annual report for the following year, President Wm. Frantz pays a glowing tribute to his predecessor, Prof. Deiler, saying that it was due to him that during the past fourteen years the attention of the whole country had been drawn to the work done by the German

Society, that Deiler's book on Louisiana had been the basis of all sub-
sequent books and articles written about Louisiana and its possibilities,
that Deiler's History of the German Society had contributed much to
acquaint the United States and Europe with this Society, by representing it in its true light as one of the oldest organizations of its kind
in this country and highly esteemed by the highest authorities of the
land.   Mr. Frantz speaks of Prof. Deiler's manly appearance, his energetic, yet amiable demeanor, his penetrating but pleasing voice and
his choice eloquence.   He says that the Society would not easily find
another president like Prof. Deiler, a man who combined the best
qualities of the German and of the American, a man of many attainments, highly cultured in music, literature and historic research, ever
ready to give and to do his best for the German Society.

Mr. Wm. Frantz continued in the office of president of the German
Society till 1922, when he was made an honorary member.   He is still
an active member, in spite of his advanced age of 82 years, and highly
respected and beloved.

Teaching of German in the Public Schools

Dr. John C. Ransmeier came to Tulane in 1907 to take charge of
the German Department, replacing Prof. Deiler.   Under his leadership,
German soon became one of the most popular subjects in the University.   He continued at Tulane until the World War, when German
was discontinued.   Dr. Ransmeier and Jos. Reuther, president of the
German Society, were instrumental in introducing the teaching of
German into the public schools, as a regular subject in the high schools
and an extra-class subject in the grade schools in the afternoons.
Largely through Dr. Ransmeier's influence, the German Society gave
annual prizes to the pupils most proficient in German in the high
schools.

The annual report for 1915 gives a list of seven high schools, with
the names of the pupils who won prizes, and the books given.

The German Society also donated to the various high schools
libraries of 100 volumes each, including classics, books on history and
histories of literature.

To provide teachers of German in two of our public schools which
were fostered by the German Society, Mr. Sigmund Odenheimer contributed over $2,000.

Activities During the World War and Since

Before the United States entered the war, five transports of German
refugee women and children from East Asia, and one of German
colonial officers from the German South Sea Islands passed through
New Orleans on their way home and were welcomed by the Germans
of this city and representatives of the German Society distributed

refreshments among them, especially fruit and chocolates for the children.

A meeting was held in which Irish Americans joined with those of German descent to protest against the exportation of arms and ammunition to belligerent countries at war with Germany.

A great bazaar was given in the Athenaeum on April 28 and 29, 1915, for the benefit of the German and Austrian Red Cross, in the preparation of which our Mr. Forchheimer was the leading spirit. On the first night 2,500 people attended, while on the second night about 4,000 literally jammed the auditorium and its booths, including many full-blooded Americans. The proceeds netted about $7,000. This was by far the greatest German success in the history of New Orleans in the way of benevolent co-operation.

Two notable speakers from Germany visited our city during this period. Prof. Eugene Kühnemann, of the University of Breslau, had been delivering lectures throughout this country, mainly in English, about the war, and had everywhere captured his hearers by his eloquence. In our city he also gave a lecture in German on Goethe's Faust, with recitations from memory of large parts of that drama. As Professor of History of German Literature, he was especially qualified to treat this subject. Those who heard him will remember what a rich treat it was.

The other visitor from Germany was a woman, Miss Schmidt-Pauli. She addressed the members and friends of the German Society on October 19, 1916, in the gold room of the Grunewald Hotel, in the interest of the East Prussia Relief. Her address in German was one of matchless beauty and eloquence. Although no collection had been announced, a spontaneous offering was made by those present, of $113, for the cause for which she pleaded.

The sufferings of the thousands of people in Germany during the period immediately following the Armistice, through loss of their property on account of the depreciation of German money, as well as the deaths of so many breadwinners during the war, aroused the sympathetic hearts not only of the Germans in this country, but of many who had no German blood in their veins.

Already in 1918, Col. John P. Mayo, Commissioner of Immigration, asked and received aid from the German Society for the officers and sailors interned in the Immigration Station. United States Attorney Jos. W. Montgomery asked and obtained the assistance of the Society in placing German prisoners whom he desired to liberate.

In 1920 the Society donated $100 to the organization which Mrs. J. A. Storck had formed for the relief of the war sufferers in Germany, and when a Mr. Nicholson of Philadelphia, a representative of the Quakers, who did such a noble work for the poor and under-nourished children in Germany, appeared before the German Society appealing for these unfortunates, the Society contributed $250 towards this relief work, and its president, Wm. Edenborn, added a personal gift of $50. These funds were transmitted by Mrs. Storck.

During the following year the German Society inaugurated an Aid Committee, under the name of "German and Austrian Destitute Relief Commission of New Orleans," consisting of the following gentlemen: Jos. Reuther, chairman; Paul Schwartz, secretary; Wm. Edenborn, treasurer; S. Odenheimer, ex-officio; P. Abele, F. Baldenhofer, E. Bornemann, Wm. Frantz, H. B. Gessner, M. D.; Wm. Groh, Rev. Max Heller, Ferd. Koelle, Frank Landsee, Wm. Moellenkamp, F. Molitor, Max Pfister, Bruno Prager, Max Schmidt, Ludwig Schulz, Sr., G. Seybold, Geo. Springer, Jacob Thomas, Chas. Wirth.

The German Society requested steamship companies whose ships entered our port to appoint a physician able to speak the German language, and upon this request Dr. J. Marcus Koelle was appointed by four such companies in 1922.

Upon the statement of Director C. F. Helmecke that immigrants bound for New Orleans, in passing through Havana, had been persuaded by consuls or ship agents to change their route and enter this country through Mexico, and as their passports designated New Orleans as their destination, admission to the United States was denied them, except through this port, the German Society requested Attorney Helmecke to take steps to remedy this evil.

In 1924, President Jos. Reuther reports that in view of the appalling conditions in the Fatherland, the Germans of New Orleans, under the auspices of the German Society, raised the past year the sum of almost $2,400 to aid in relieving the distress. For this sum, 1,000 sacks of rice were sent to Germany and distributed by the Red Cross of Berlin. Receipts and letters of thanks were received from all parts of Germany.

The Society also aided the German storm sufferers in Florida in 1926.

A banquet was arranged at the suggestion of the German Society in honor of Wm. Edenborn, on May 11, 1924, which was largely attended. More recently a banquet was given in honor of the visiting German Ambassador, Baron Ago von Maltzan, under the auspices of the German Society, and with an enthusiastic attendance of large numbers of Germans of New Orleans and their friends, on March 18, 1927. Addresses were made by Wm. Frantz, E. F. Koelle, Monsignor J. Francis Prim and Rev. Louis Voss, D. D., with a gracious response by the Ambassador. His recent tragic death in an airplane accident cast a pall of sorrow over his many friends here and elsewhere. He was spoken of as the greatest diplomat Germany ever sent to this country.

During all these recent years and up to the present time, the German Society has maintained its work of securing employment for such Germans as applied to it, and of bestowing benevolence on those in need. In every annual report figures running into the hundreds are given of such as were aided by meals and lodging or by cash donations. Advice and information were given to all who inquired in person and in response to letters received from many parts of the world.

LIST OF THE OFFICERS DURING THE PAST EIGHTY YEARS

PRESIDENTS

Wilh. Vogel	1847-1852
J. H. Eimer	1853-1855
F. W. Freudenthal	
	1856, 1858-1861
Wilh. De la Rue	1861-1873
Fr. Rickert	1873-1890
H. F. Klumpp	1890-1891
Carl Wernicke	1891-1893
Jos. Brandner	1893-1895
J. Hanno Deiler	1895-1909
Wm. Frantz	1910-1914
Dr. P. Roh	1915-1916
Hans Forchheimer	1916-1917
Dr. H. A. Gabert	1918-1921
Jos. Reuther	1922-1927

Dr. B. Maas	1857-1859
A. Hasche	1859-1862
C. Bendix	1862-1863
C. Theo. Foerster	1863-1865
C. Bendix	1865-1874
H. F. Klumpp	1874-1890
Otto Knoop	1890-1895
E. F. Del Bondio	1895-1905
G. Ad. Blaffer	1905-1910
Julius Koch	1910-1912
Dr. H. A. Gabert	1912-1913
Jos. Voegtle	1913-1916
Wm. Edenborn	1916-1926
Frank Langbehn	1927

FIRST VICE-PRESIDENTS

J. H. Eimer	1847-1852
F. W. Freudenthal	1852-1855
H. F. Zernicke	1855-1856
S. Schmidt	1856-1857
Fr. Rickert	1857-1861
" "	1870-1873
W. Thiel	1861-1863
Jos. Lang	1863-1864
E. S. Würzburger	1873-1875
Jos. Brandner	1875-1893
Wm. Frantz	1893-1909
Otto Walther	1909-1912
Julius Koch	1912-1913
Dr. H. A. Gabert	1913-1915
" " "	1917-1918
Jos. Reuther	1915-1916
Geo. Ehrhard	1917-1921
Bruno Prager	1921-1927

SECOND VICE-PRESIDENTS

Dr. E. Authenried	1847-1848
F. W. Freudenthal	1848-1852
C. T. Buddecke	1852-1855
E. Rodewald	1855-1856
W. Thiel	1856-1857

TREASURERS

J. D. Kamper	1847-1848
C. v. Voigts	1848-1850
Geo. Dirmeyer	1850-1851
" "	1852-1859
J. A. Blaffer	1859-1860
E. Claren	1860-1861
" "	1862-1863
H. F. Stürcken	1861-1862
W. B. Schmidt	1862-1871
J. W. Buhrmann	1871-1879
Ph. W. Dielmann	1879-1895
G. Ad. Blaffer	1895-1905
O. T. Maier	1905-1911
Emil Pier	1911-1916
Phil. I. Adam	1916-1921
Dr. J. M. Koelle	1922-1927

RECORDING SECRETARIES

J. F. Behnke	1847-1848
Aug. Schneider	1848-1849
" "	1850-1851
S. Runkel	1849-1850
H. F. Zernicke	1851-1853
H. Goldmann	1853-1855
E. Claren	1855-1858
L. Schwartz	1858-1860
" "	1862-1882

J. W. Buhrmann	1882-1886	Wm. De la Rue	1851-1855
J. Hanno Deiler	1886-1891	" "	1856-1861
" "	1894-1895	G. L. L. Meyer	1855-1856
John Köper	1891-1893	Th. Runde	1861-1862
Otto Walther	1893-1908	J. Marschall	1862-1863
P. J. Sendker	1909-1916	C. Strieder	1863-1864
F. C. Mundhenke	1916-1917	F. Froh	1864-1874
Paul Schwartz	1917-1927	F. W. Seiler	1874-1877
		M. Vonderbank	1877-1891
FINANCIAL SECRETARIES		Ed. Eitzen	1891-1903
Aug. Schneider	1847-1848	Aug. Schmedtje	1903-1916
Rud. Schlothe	1848-1849	A. W. Euler	1916-1917
L. Schmidt	1849-1850	Otto Gottscho	1916-1918
K. Buff	1850-1851	Jos. Engel	1923-1927

Wilh. De la Rue, Financial Secretary from 1851 to 1861, and President from 1861 to 1873, was born in 1800, at Erlangen, Bavaria, and attained an age of 72 years, 50 of which he spent in America and 40 in New Orleans. During the Mexican War he served as officer of the U. S. Army. Later he became a commission merchant. At the outbreak of the Civil War the firm of De La Rue & Sloan was dissolved and Mr. De la Rue, who was afflicted with an ear trouble which caused complete deafness, retired from business. Of him, the 26th annual report of the German Society says that during his long term as president he was a staunch friend of the immigrants, and highly respected by all his fellow citizens.

H. F. Klumpp, president from 1890 to 1891, for 30 years a member, 4 years a director and 15 years second vice president, died on December 31, 1894. He was a man of strict integrity, a noble character and amiable disposition. His long and faithful service to the German Society entitle him to our lasting and honorable memory.

William Frantz beheld the light of day February 24, 1845, in that modest and humble Alsace-Lorraine village, Wiebersviller, nestled along one of the many small streams running through that section of the country. His ancestors were wall and tower clock makers; but when the Black Forest clock industry developed, his forefathers gave up this industry, fostered for generations back, and became village blacksmiths. In the early spring of 1857, his parents emigrated to New Orleans with their three sons, seven, ten and twelve years of age, respectively.

Those were the days when the most dreaded of all dreaded visitations came upon New Orleans, at periods separated by only a few years. One year after their arrival New Orleans was visited by one of those distressing epidemics. The Frantz family occupied one room, sparsely furnished. A chest brought from the old country served as an armoire, table and chairs. At meals the children would kneel before the chest, the parents sitting at either end. The dreaded scourge entered that humble immigrant's home, the inhabitants of which, one after another, became its victims, waiting on each other as best they could. That noble and benevolent organization, the Howard Association, sent its physician and supplied the medicine, and by the providence of God they all recovered. The faithful attending physician, a graduate of the Louisiana Medical University, having just returned from Paris, where he had taken a post graduate course, was stricken, and in spite of the best medical attention and all possible nursing and care, died.

Mr. Frantz, in May, 1867, married Miss Wilhelmina D. Koepf, whose father was a Swabian and a veteran of the Texas War for Independence. Eight children blessed their marital life. One died in its infancy, another at the age of twenty-two years. Their three sons and three daughters married and established their own homes.

Mr. Frantz started in business September 1, 1874, with nothing but his mechanical profession, gradually working his way to Canal street, and then to Carondelet street, where the firm is still located. He retired seven years ago, and two of his sons, with two of their friends, carry on the business.

Mr. Frantz was one of the organizers of the second oldest homestead association in the city and at present is the president of the Third District Building (Homestead) Association, and was a member of its first board of directors. He was likewise a member of the first board of directors of the Protestant Home for the Aged; its vice president and its president for years. He served for twenty years as a member of the Orleans Parish School Board. He became a member of the German Society in 1877; was a member of its board of directors from 1882 to 1893, when he became its vice president to 1911 and president to 1915. On retiring he was made an honorary member. A picture of Mr. Frantz appears on page 7.

Joseph Voegtle was born in Freiburg, Baden, February 26, 1853. Came to New Orleans in 1870. Became manager and proprietor of the Cosmopolitan Hotel. Was a member of the New Orleans Sewerage and Water Board. Served as Senator in the Louisiana Legislature. Became a member of the German Society, and served as Second Vice President from 1913 to 1916, and as Director from 1895 to his death. Was a Director of the German Protestant Orphan Asylum and Chairman of its House Committee. Was one of the organizers and president of the "Frohsinn," a German singing society. Was a director of the Canal Bank, and Postmaster of New Orleans from 1914 to 1916. Took an active part in social and philanthropic movements, liberal in his contributions, courteous and obliging.

CONCLUSION

The writer has lived in this city for the past 47 years as the pastor of a church originally German in its membership and services, though now thoroughly Americanized. The use of the German language in its services was discontinued long before the World War, there being no further need of it. To hold the young people, it was necessary to use the common language of the people, an illustration of the best method of Americanizing foreigners.

The writer is also the sole surviving charter member of the German Protestant Home for the Aged and Infirm, which looks back upon a history of forty years. He has taken an active part in all matters concerning the welfare of our people and especially his own people. A native of Germany, he has ever identified himself with those of the same origin and has sought to uphold their best ideals of integrity and thrift, their aspirations in music and literature, and their loyalty to their adopted country. He feels that he has some right to speak in behalf of the present generation of Germans and their descendants now living in New Orleans, and that he expresses their sentiments, as well as his own, when he acknowledges the debt of gratitude they owe to those splendid men who for eighty years have carried on the self-denying work of the German Society. And with this expression of thanks he bespeaks their continued loyal support and encouragement of the work of the German Society.

———

The German Society, in its eighty years of unselfish and altruistic work, has assisted thousands upon thousands of stranded and needy individuals and numbers of families; secured employment, given needful advice, also transportation. In special, pressing conditions, such as the Galveston storm, epidemics and other disasters, it always lent a helping hand.

Has the German Society fulfilled its mission? Let us be thankful for what it has done in these eighty years of helping others; and if it still has a future work to do, let us not withhold our co-operation and help.

ADDENDUM

August Hoppe acted as agent of the German Society during the yellow fever epidemic of 1853, as stated on page 80. He was born October 19, 1818, at Asch, in Bohemia, and came to New Orleans in 1842. He enlisted in the Mexican War, after which he joined Buffalo Bill in hunting buffaloes. In 1848 he returned to Germany to get his wife and two daughters. The youngest of these, Widow Ernestine Gaschen, now 86 years old, is still living with her daughter, the wife of Rev. Louis Voss.

Carl Becker acted as agent of the German Society for twenty years and enjoyed its fullest confidence. He died March 15, 1890. His successor was Leopold Grube, who served for seven years. He died in November, 1897.

Louis Bermes was agent from 1897 to 1917; G. E. Seybold in 1917, and Paul Schwartz from 1918 to 1923.

This Appendix contains several articles dealing with Prof. J. Hanno Deiler. The first appeared in *Deutsch-Amerikanische Geschichtsblätter*, 9:4(1909): 158-59; the second appeared in *Americana Germanica*, 11:5(1909): 277-79; and the third in *American-German Review*, 8:3(1942): 25-27.

† Profeſſor J. Hanno Deiler.

Profeſſor J. Hanno Deiler.

Am 20. Juli d. J. iſt in Covington in
Louiſiana Herr J. Hanno Deiler ge-
ſtorben, einer der hervorragendſten Erfor-
ſcher deutſch-amerikaniſcher Geſchichte, und
zuletzt, bis Kränklichkeit ihn zwang, ſein
Amt niederzulegen, Profeſſor der deutſchen
Sprache und Literatur an der Univerſität
Tulane in New Orleans. Geboren im
Auguſt 1849 in Alt-Oetting in Bayern,
war er, nachdem er die polytechniſche Schule
in München durchgemacht hatte, im Jahre
1872 nach New Orleans gekommen, wo er
ſehr bald mit der Leitung des deutſchen
Unterrichts in den öffentlichen Schulen be-
traut wurde; in den achtziger Jahren er-
folgte ſeine Berufung auf den Stuhl der
deutſchen Sprache und Literatur an der
obengenannten Univerſität. Wie er in die-
ſer Stellung der akademiſchen Jugend des
Südens das Verſtändniß für deutſche Literatur und deutſchen Geiſt öffnete, wirkte er
als Mitarbeiter und wenn wir nicht irren
auch Mitbeſitzer der „Deutſchen Zeitung"
in New Orleans eifrig an der Aufrecht-
erhaltung deutſcher Sprache, deutſchen Sin-

nes und deutscher Sitte seitens der einge-
wanderten Deutschen in seiner näheren und
ferneren Umgebung, und als Präsident der
Deutschen Gesellschaft von New Orleans
für den Schutz der deutschen Einwanderer,
und wurde in Anerkennung seiner Verdienste in diesen Richtungen und seiner
glänzenden Rednergabe mehrfach zum Prä-
sidenten des Nationalen deutsch-amerikani-
schen Sängerbundes gewählt.

Sein Hauptverdienst aber um das
Deutschthum, und dasjenige, was seinen
Namen auf ferne Nachwelt tragen wird, ist
die von ihm mit großer Liebe und persön-
licher Anstrengung ausgeführte Erforschung
der Geschichte der deutschen Einwanderung
in Louisiana. Als Frucht dieser Forschungen sind von ihm im Druck erschienen: „Das
Redemptionssystem im Staat Louisiana";
„Geschichte der deutschen Kirchengemeinden
in Louisiana"; „Geschichte der deutschen
Einwanderung von 1820 bis 1896"; „Geschichte der Deutschen Gesellschaft von New
Orleans"; „Geschichte der deutschen Presse
in New Orleans"; „Eine vergessene deutsche Kolonie"; „Die deutsche Sprache und
deutsche Familien-Namen unter den Kreo-
len von Louisiana", und noch im letzten
Jahre in den „German American Annals" „Die Besiedlung der deutschen Küste
von Louisiana". Besonders werthvoll sind
seine Forschungen über den Wechsel, welchen
die deutschen Namen nacheinander unter
französischer, spanischer und amerikanischer
Herrschaft durchgemacht haben.

Wir vermuthen, daß in seinem Nachlaß noch manches bisher Unveröffentlichtes ist, was hoffentlich seine Familie in den Druck bringt.

Sein frühes Hinscheiden ist ein schwerer Verlust für das Deutschthum und die deutsch-amerikanische Forschung.

102

J. HANNO DEILER. *Eine Würdigung.*

Die Nachricht, dass J. Hanno Deiler, Professor Emeritus der Tulane Universität in New Orleans, in Covington, La., in dessen Fichtenwäldern er eine Besserung seines Herzleidens erhoffte, am 21. Juli gestorben ist, hat nicht allein in Deutsch-Amerika, sondern auch in den amerikanischen Kreisen, in welchen man die Verdienste deutsch-amerikanischer Geschichtsforscher zu schätzen weiss, aufrichtige Trauer hervorgerufen.

Deiler war bahnbrechend für die Erforschung der Geschichte der deutschen Einwanderung am unteren Mississippi gewesen. In französischen Quellen, in alten Kirchenbüchern, in den überaus dürftigen Überlieferungen, welche eine schriftliche Aufzeichnung gefunden haben und bis auf unsere Zeit erhalten geblieben sind, suchte er mühsam das Material zusammen und ordnete es zu dem lichtvollen und hochinteressanten Essay, der in den "GERMAN AMERICAN ANNALS" unter dem Titel "The Settlement of the German Coast of Louisiana" kürzlich erschien und dessen Buchausgabe jetzt fertiggestellt ist. Was amerikanische Geschichtsschreiber, wenn sie es überhaupt einer Erwähnung würdigten, ganz kurz berührten, das hatte Hanno Deiler zum Gegenstande eingehender Studien gemacht und eine völlige "terra incognita" geschichtlicher Forschung erschlossen. Ohne ihn wäre wohl nie bekannt geworden, dass deutscher Energie und deutschem Fleisse die Durchführung eines kolonialen Unternehmens zu danken ist, an welchem französische Ansiedlungsversuche scheiterten. Bei der Urbarmachung der fast undurchdringlichen Cypressenwälder unter der tropischen Sonne des Südens bewährten sich die Deutschen als erfolgreiche Pioniere. Und was sie einmal dem jungfräulichen Boden in schwerer, ermüdernder und langwieriger Arbeit abgerungen hatten, das behaupteten sie trotz der Zerstörungslust der Elemente und der Feindseligkeit der Indianer. Ansiedlungen, deren ursprünglich deutsche Namen durch französische und spanische Spracheinflüsse vollständig unerkennbar geworden waren, wusste Deiler mit grossem Scharfsinn als deutsch zu reklamieren. Seine Abhandlung über "Die Creolen deutscher Abstammung" ist eine ethnographische Studie, in welcher er den Nachweiss führt, dass nicht allein die in Louisiana geborenen

J. Hanno Deiler

Söhne und Töchter französischer und spanischer Eltern als Creolen bezeichnet wurden, sondern auch die Kinder deutscher Eltern.

Interessante Beiträge zur Geschichte des Deutschtums in New Orleans bot Deiler in seiner "Geschichte der New Orleanser deutschen Presse" und in seiner "Geschichte der Deutschen Gesellschaft von New Orleans". Leider ist der zweite Teil der "Geschichte der deutschen Presse" nicht vollendet. Hanno Deiler schrieb in einem elf Tage vor seinem Tode an den Unterzeichneten gerichteten Briefe: "Der zweite Teil meiner "Geschichte der deutschen Presse" ist noch nicht fertig, da ich das Material für manche der Denkwürdigkeiten, die ich, wie im ersten Teil, hineinarbeiten will, bisher nich habe zusammenbringen können. Meine lange Krankheit, ich liege seit dem 3. Juni beinahe beständig im Bett und soll weder lesen oder schreiben, noch denken, ist Schuld daran".

Über die Zahl und den Bestand deutscher Kirchen und Schulen gibt Deiler in seiner "Geschichte der deutschen Kirchengemeinden im Staate Louisiana" Aufschluss. Als Vorkämpfer des Deutschtums verrichteten deutsche katholische und protestantische Geistliche dieselbe schwere Arbeit zur Erschliessung des Bodens, wie die irischen Glaubensboten in den Wäldern Germaniens. Vom Zauber amerikanischer Siedlungsromantik getragen, wird Deilers Ehrenrettung des geheimnissvollen Führers deutscher Schwärmer, des Grafen Maximilian de Leon, alias Proli, alias Bernhard Müller, aus Offenbach, den die Rappisten, angeblich fälschlich, zum Schwindler stempelten, weil ihnen die neue Ansiedlung in ihrer Nähe, welche im Jahre 1837 von Proli in Philippsburg, Pa., angelegt worden war, nicht gefiel. Der deutsche Kaiser erkannte Deilers verdienstvolle Forscherarbeit dadurch an, dass er ihm den Kronenorden verlieh.

Aber Deiler war nicht allein ein Geschichtsforscher von bahnbrechender Bedeutung, ein Jugendbildner, der während seiner 28-jährigen Lehrtätigkeit unter den Studenten der Tulane Universität der deutschen Sprache und Literatur viele Freunde gewonnen hat, ein Redner von geradezu packender Wirkung, wenn es der deutschen Sache galt, ein begeisterter Vorkämpfer des deutschen Liedes, dem er als ausgezeichneter Dirigent und als Präsident des Nordamerikanischen Sängerbundes seine Dienste widmete, sondern auch ein stolzer Verkünder des Wertes und der Bedeutung der deutschen Einwanderung unter dem Amerikanertum, das ihm, dem hervorragenden Gelehrten und berufenen Führer des Deutschtums, den Zoll der Anerkennung und Hochachtung nicht versagen konnte. Es ist nicht mit Unrecht behauptet worden, dass der Tod Hanno Deilers einen schwer zu ersetzenden Verlust für Deutsch-Amerika bedeutet, denn von ihm ging eine Menge wertvoller Anregungen aus, deren Durchführung dem deutschen Element in den Vereinigten Staaten zum Heile gereichte. Hanno Deiler hat das 60ste Lebensjahr nicht vollendet. Er hatte seinem Körper zu viel zugemutet, als er in der Vollkraft seiner Jahre stand und seine Lebensenergie aufgebraucht, um dem Deutschtum und der deutschen Sache zu dienen. Wenn der Besten deutschen Stammes hier in Amerika gedacht wird, wird der Mann nicht vergessen werden, der die grossen Verdienste der deutschen Einwanderung am unteren Mississippi nachwies und so viel getan hat, um in seinen Landsleuten den Stolz auf die deutsche Abstammung zu erwecken und mächtig anzuregen.

Nachstehend eine kurze biographische Skizze, welche in dem nahezu fertiggestellten Werke "Das Buch der Deutschen in Amerika" erscheinen wird und die Gutheissung Hanno Deilers gefunden hat:

Johann Hanno Deiler wurde am 8. August, 1849, in Altötting, Ober-Bayern, geboren, war Schullehrer in Bayern und wurde 1871 als Vorsteher an eine deutsche Schule in New Orleans berufen. Er landete am 22. Januar, 1872, in New York. Im Jahre 1879 wurde er Professor an der University of Louisiana (jetzt Tulane Universität). Er liess sich hie Pflege des deutschen Männergesangs unter seinen Landsleuten in New Orleans angelegen sein und suchte fördernd auf deren geistiges Leben einzuwirken. Eine Reihe von Jahren war er Präsident der Deutschen Gesellschaft in der Halbmondstadt. Er gründete den New Orleans Quartett Club, einen der besten Gesang-Vereine des Südens. Da er selbst musikalisch gebildet war, wurde er dessen Dirigent. Prof. Deiler leitete die Massenchöre beim grossen Sängerfest des Nordamerikanischen Sängerbundes im Februar 1890 in New Orleans, welches zu einem grossartigen Erfolge sich gestaltete. Prof. Deiler wohnte dem 4. Allgemeinen Deutschen Sängerbundfest in Wien 1890 und dem 5. in Stuttgart 1896 bei und fand als Redner eine geradezu enthusiastische Aufnahme. Seit 1890 war er Präsident des Nordamerikanischen Sängerbundes. Er gründete das Archiv für deutsche Geschichte. Im Jahre 1907 legte er Krankheit halber sein Amt als Professor der deutschen Sprache und Literatur an der Tulane Universität, das er 28 Jahre in verdienstvoller Weise bekleidet hatte, nieder.

MAX HEINRICI.

J. Hanno Deiler

Cultural Pioneer of the South

By ARTHUR H. MOEHLENBROCK

As EDUCATOR, musician, organizer of choirs and philharmonic societies, civic leader, sociologist, author, and historian, J. Hanno Deiler was one of the most distinguished figures in the cultural life of the South in the last quarter of the nineteenth century. To-day the historical records from the pen of Professor Deiler constitute the most reliable and the most abundant source material on *Germanica Americana* in Louisiana.

Professor Deiler was born at Altoetting, Bavaria, August 8, 1849, and named John Hanno, though he usually signed his name J. Hanno Deiler. His father, Conrad Deiler, was a royal court musician and a descendant of an ancient family of Nuremberg, where his ancestors are mentioned as early as 1400 as "Genannte," that is, members of the "Grosse Rat." J. Hanno and his older brother, Aloys, attended the public school in Altoetting. In their early youth, both received musical training from their father, who was director of the choir of the Holy Chapel there, and from Anton Mueller, the Royal Chapel master and composer.

At the age of ten, J. Hanno's soprano voice was recognized as excellent, and, though so young, he was appointed soloist of the Choir of St. Emmeran, at Regensburg. The young singer also received a scholarship in the "Studien- und Musik-Seminar," which enabled him to study at the Royal Gymnasium without expense to his parents. The records mention that he won prizes every season. At the age of seventeen he was awarded a second scholarship, which enabled him to study at the Royal Normal College of Munich, where he was graduated at the age of nineteen, with honors in every branch of study.

Young Deiler arrived in America on New Year's Day, 1872, at the age of twenty-three. That year was the beginning of a brilliant career as a German-American educator in the South. Also in December of that year he married Wilhelmina Saganowsky, daughter of Paul Saganowsky, an engineer.

For four years before coming to America Deiler had held government appointments as teacher, the last of which was at the Model School of the City of Munich. During that period he pursued advanced studies in German literature, history, esthetics, and related subjects at the Royal Polytechnic Institute. In New Orleans he was teacher of German in parochial schools for seven years. For a while he served as many as five schools at one time.

In 1879 he became Professor of German at Tulane University, which at that time was called the University of Louisiana. During his twenty-seven years of teaching at Tulane he was known for his unbounded energy, his genial attitude toward students, and his untiring enthusiasm for creating interest in his native language and literature. He gained the reputation of being a man of research with many outside activities, who, nevertheless, had time to be patient and sympathetic toward the individual student. For some years he not only taught his classes by day, but operated a free night school in order to encourage the study of German.

From his youth he had been an enthusiastic singer, and a love for vocal music continued to play a vital part in his entire life. His greatest honor as a musician was that of becoming the director of the North American Saengerbund.

In 1872 Deiler became organist of St. Boniface Church at New Orleans. A month after his arrival in the city he became a member of the German "Maennergesangverein," which had been organized but a short time before. Deiler was the director of that society for two years. In 1874 he went to Cincinnati and for six months directed the "Maennergesang" section of the "Cincinnati Maennerchor."

In New Orleans, in 1880, eighteen months after the fusion of the "German Maennergesangverein" with the "Liederkranz," Professor Deiler became the director. He also organized the first German mixed chorus in Louisiana, and directed the grand concerts organized by the "Liedertafel" at Spanish Fort and West End in honor of the Texan Singers present to celebrate the opening of railroad communications with Texas, in October, 1880.

On August 8, 1882, Professor Deiler, with seven others, founded the New Orleans Quartette Club. A year later he traveled to Buffalo making contact with the Northern singers for the first time. In 1884, he accompanied the Club to San Antonio to visit the "Beethoven Maennerchor," which arranged a concert on August 6th. On that occasion the New Orleans organization won its first laurels outside its own city. In 1886 the Club appeared at the Saengerfest in Milwaukee with a double quartette. Here they won unusual applause, and decided to join the North American Saengerbund. This was the fulfillment of the underlying purpose for which Deiler had organized the Quartette Club.

In 1888, forty singers from New Orleans, under the leadership of Deiler, attended the twenty-fifth Saengerfest which met at St. Louis. They made so great an impression that a unanimous vote was given to meet at New Orleans for the next national festival two years later. Professor Deiler was made Festival Director and Chairman of the Music Committee, and proved to be the leading spirit in making the first national music festival in the South a great success.

Deiler's work through the German Society constituted the greater part of his civic service to the State of Louisiana. When he joined the Society in 1879 he found it at its lowest ebb. Its membership having dwindled from some four hundred to only seventy-four, it was practically ready to disband. The Society had begun to believe that it had accomplished its original purposes— (1) to aid immigrants in landing, (2) to assist those who were bound for the North and West in continuing their journey on up the Mississippi River, and (3) to help find employment for those who were planning to remain in New Orleans or elsewhere in Louisiana. Since German immigration to New Orleans had decreased in numbers from as many as 40,000 in 1854 to as few as two persons in 1875-76, it is no wonder that their original program of service had been altered. But Deiler felt the need of preserving the history of the Germans who had come to this country by the Southern route. As secretary of the German Society he had had occasion to collect statistics which showed that nearly 300,000 Germans had landed in New Orleans within the forty-year period between 1847 and 1887. In 1889 he proposed "the creation of an Archive and Library Committee to gather material bearing on the history of the Germans on the Lower Mississippi." This resulted in the gathering and listing of many hundred books and pamphlets.

Deiler's practical business sense and power of leadership were evidenced more and more in the records of the Society's activities, among which were numerous benefits to convalescent homes and homes for the aged and infirm.

In 1907, J. Hanno Deiler and Charles Schuler, Commissioner of Agriculture and Immigration, made a trip to Germany for the definite purpose of spreading "correct knowledge concerning the State of Louisiana among the people of the Fatherland." Their efforts were intended neither to solicit nor to discourage departure from the home country, but to influence those who were emigrating to make Louisiana their new home.

The German people received the two men with enthusiasm and seemed to welcome the speeches that Deiler made in his native tongue, bringing them authentic information about the State of Louisiana. An essay by the German pastor, Voss, of New Orleans, published with the approval of Deiler and Schuler, was made available to the hitherto uniformed German peasants. A sample paragraph from that essay shows why prospective immigrants were able to place confidence in the representatives from New Orleans:

"Whoever can secure a livelihood in the old country should not emigrate, but many are forced by necessity or unfavorable conditions to leave the Fatherland. To such people who wish or may be forced to find a new home in another hemisphere, and cast their eyes in the direction of the United States of America, the State of Louisiana may be a welcome haven. There is in that State . . . fertile land . . . waterways . . . mild climate . . . comfortable existence. True, the colonists must have some means in order to pay the first installment on the lands they wish to acquire, as well as to secure costs of the first seeding, . . . fences . . . dwellings, . . . until they can harvest their first crop. This requires a sum of about 2,000 marks . . . "

Sharecropping, also, was explained for those who had no money for their first year's set-up in a new country.

That was Deiler's last trip back to the old country, as the remaining two years of his life were fully occupied with travel throughout the State of Louisiana in an endeavor to collect all the data possible for his history of the Germans who had settled in that State. A member of the German Society for thirty years, its recording secretary for five, its president for fourteen, Professor Deiler was in position to know where to go for first-hand information for much of that history.

When the Historical Society of Louisiana obtained copies of documents from the Marine Archives in Paris for Professor Deiler to use in completing the history of Germans in Louisiana, he gave up teaching at Tulane University in order to devote his full time to research. Two years later, 1909, shortly before the author's death, the book was submitted to the press under the title, *The Settlement of the German Coast of Louisiana and the Creoles of German Descent,* and was published in Philadelphia, New York, Berlin, Leipzig, London, and Paris.

His book, *Louisiana, a Home for German Settlers,* written some years earlier, had been published, 10,000 copies in German and 100,000 in English. It stimulated widespread inquiry about the State and influenced numbers of German families to leave other places in the United States and move to Louisiana.

He wrote several other important books on phases of the history of Germans in the lower Mississippi region, a description of the German churches of New Orleans, and a study of German immigration from 1820 to 1900.

Professor Deiler has been described by some who knew him personally as having a manly appearance, an energetic, yet amiable demeanor, and a penetrating but pleasing voice. On his last visit to Germany he was honored not only by the people, but also by their ruler, Emperor William II, who made Deiler a Knight of the Crown.

When he died suddenly on July 20, 1909, tributes from all over the country indicated how wide had been Deiler's influence, especially in the fields of music and historical research. As one of his colleagues expressed it, Professor Deiler was a man of many attainments, who combined the best qualities of the German and the American.

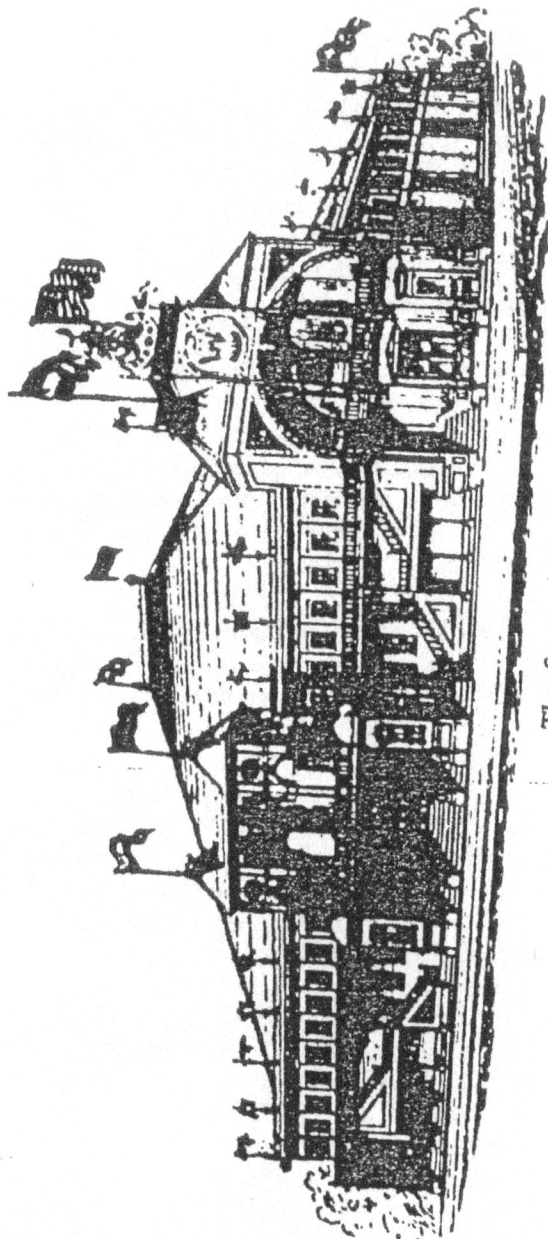

The Saengerhalle
located at Lee Circle, New Orleans, La.
It was built under Deiler's supervision especially to house the first national music festival
but it is no longer standing.

Notes:

Editor's Preface:

1. This work was originally published as: *History of the German Society of New Orleans, With an Introduction Giving a Synopsis of the History of the Germans in the United States, With Special Reference to those in Louisiana, Written at the Request of the German Society and Published by it on the Occasion of its Eightieth Anniversary, Celebrated on December 6, 1927,* (New Orleans: Sendker Printing Service, Inc., 1927).

2. See my discussion of "German-American Studies, 1492 to 1992 and Beyond" in Don Heinrich Tolzmann, *Germany and America:, 1450-1700: Julius Friedrich Sachse's History of the German Role in the Discovery, Exploration, and Settlement of the New World,* (Bowie, MD: Heritage Books, Inc., 1991), pp. 16-28.

Editor's Introduction:

1. See Don Heinrich Tolzmann, "1990 Census Statististics," *Society for German-American Studies Newsletter,* (14:1(1993): 6-7.

2. John Frederick Nau, *The German People of New Orleans, 1850-1900,* (Leiden: E.J. Brill, 1958), p. xiii.

3. Ibid. Voss refers to the "inadequate" treatment of the role of German-Americans in American history (pp. 44ff), and thereby identifies a major problem and paradox in American historical writing, namely, how one-fourth of the American population receives rarely more than a brief mention. In the 1890s, Julius Friedrich Sachse had written that "Writers of American history have thus far failed to accord" to Germans "anything like the proper amount of credit due them..." He

114

also notes that "Instances are extremely rare where the average historian has accorded any credit to the German people in connection with the history of this country." See Don Heinrich Tolzmann, *Germany and America, 1450-1700: Julius Friedrich Sachse's History of the German Role in the Discovery, Exploration, and Settlement of the New World,* (Bowie, MD: Heritage Books, Inc., 1991), pp. 33-34. H.M.M. Richards noted that since German-Americans have played a significant role in American history, and that one would, hence, expect to find there history adequately recorded, but notes that "As we return, with expectant interest, to the pages of history, to learn somewhat of the character of these deeds, we are astonished to find them unrecorded." This leads to the false conclusion that "the German element of this country has been practically a nonentity" in the development of this country. See Don Heinrich Tolzmann, *German--Americans in the American Revolution: Henry Melchior Muhlenberg Richards' History,* (Bowie, MD: Heritage Books, Inc., 1992), pp. 1-2.

4. Reinhart Kondert, "Germans in Louisiana, 1720-1803," *Yearbook of German-American Studies,* 16(1981): 59. Lyle Saxon notes "Strange that historians have neglected them (the Germans) to such an extent -giving only scant notice of the tremendously important part they played in the colonization of Louisiana, and particularly the important part they played in the history of New Orleans." See Lyle Saxon, "German Pioneers in Old New Orleans," *American-German Review,* 7:3(1941): 29.

5. Regarding the German Coast, see Ellen C. Merrilll, ed., *Helmut Blume's The German Coast During the Colonial Era, 1722-1803: The Evolution of a Distinct Cultural Landscape in the Lower Mississippi Delta During the Colonial Era,* (Destrehan, Louisiana: German-Acadian Coast Historical and Genealogical Society, 1990), and Reinhart Kondert, *The Germans of Colonial Louisiana, 1720-1803,* (Stuttgart: Akademischer Verlag, 1990). Also see Hildegard Binder Johnson, *French Louisiana and the*

Development of the German Triangle: A German-American Tricentennial Publication, (Minneapolis: University of Minnesota, The Associates of the James Ford Bell Library, 1983). Saxon writes that the German Coast "was in reality the bank of the Mississippi River, beginning at a distance of perhaps twenty-five miles above New Orleans and extending for some forty miles on both banks of the stream." See Saxon, "German Pioneers," p. 29.

6. Regarding pre-1800 German books dealing with Louisiana, see Paul Baginsky, *German Works Relating to America, 1493-1800: A List Compiled from the Collections of the New York Public Library,* (New York: New York Public Library, 1942).

7. Paul C. Weber, *America in Imaginative German Literature in the First Half of the Nineteenth Century,* (New York: Columbia University Pr., 1926), p. 78. For further information on the image of the German element of Louisiana in German literature, see Aleander Ritter, *Deutschlands literarisches Amerikabild. Neuere Forschungen zur Amerikarezeption der deutschen Literatur,* (Hildesheim: Olms Verlag, 1977), pp. 204-17.

8. See Paul Wilhelm, Duke of Württemberg, *Travels inNorth America, 1822-24,* Translated by W. Robert Nitske, Edited by Savoie Lottinville, (Norman: University of Oklahoma Pr., 1973), p. 32-33, and Charles Sealsfield, *Sämtliche Werke,* Bd. 2, Hrsg. von Karl J. R. Arndt, (Hildesheim: Olms, 1972), p. 175.

9. Reizenstein's novel has been translated and edited for publication by Steven Rowan, University of Missouri-St. Louis.

10. Regarding German-American literature, see Don Heinrich Tolzmann, *German-American Literature,* (Metuchen, New Jersey: Scarecrow Pr., 1977).

116

11. Karl J.R. Arndt, *The German Language Press of the Americas: Volume 1: U.S.A.,* (München: K.G. Saur, 1976), pp. 174-75.

12. Regarding Deiler, see Nau, *The German People,* pp.

13. Erich A. Albrecht, "Deutsche Sprache, Deutsche Literatur und Deutschunterricht in New Orleans und Louisiana," *German-American Studies,* 3:1(1971): 20. For further information on the Anti-German Hysteria of World War I, see Carl Wittke, *German-Americans and the World War,* (Columbus: Ohio State Archaeological and Historical Society, 1936), and Frederick C. Luebke, *Bonds of Loyalty: German-Americans and World War I,* (DeKalb: Northern Illinois University Pr., 1974).

14. Albrecht, "Deutsche Sprache," p. 21.

15. Karl J. R. Arndt and May E. Olson, *German-American Newspapers, 1732-1955. History and Bibliography,* (Heidelberg: Quelle & Meyer, 1961). For further information about Arndt, see Don Heinrich Tolzmann, "Dr. Karl J.R. Arndt (1903-91)," *Society for German-American Studies Newsletter,* 13:1(1992): 2.

16. See Karl J.R. Arndt, "The Life of Count Leon," *American-German Review,* 6(1940): 5-8, 15-19.

17. See Karl J. R. Arndt, "The Genesis of Germantown, Louisiana," *Louisiana Historical Quarterly,* 24(1941): 378-433. Several documents pertaining to Germantown can be found in Karl J. R. Arndt, *Economy on the Ohio, 1826-1834/Ökonomie am Ohio,* (Worcester, Mass.: Harmony Society Pr., 1984).

18. Karl J.R. Arndt, *Early German-American Narratives,* (New York: American Book Co., 1941), pp.

19. Nau, *The German People,* p. 144.

20. Ibid.

21. J. Richly, *Adressbuch deutsch-amerikanischer Vereine und Gesellschaften in den USA*, (Chicago: J. Richly, 1989), pp. 151-52.

22. Regarding the work of Ellen C. Merrill, see Sevilla Finley, "German Coast History Found, Republished," *Uptown Picayune*, (31 May 1990). Bruni Mayor writes of Merrill and her outstanding contributions to the German heritage as follows: "Der Retter erschien in der Person von Dr. Ellen Merrill. In Cincinnati geboren, wo es zwar viele Deutsche gibt, hat sie trotzdem keinen Tropfen deutschen Blutes in ihren Adern. Ein Studienbesuch in Heidelberg genügte, um sie für alles Deusche einzunehmen. Die Deutschen Louisianas und New Orleans' sind somit zu ihrer Lebensaufgabe geworden, und ihre Forschungen haben ihr grosses Ansehen gebracht." See Bruni Mayor, *New Orleans* (Frankfurt am Main: Societäts-Verlag, 1992), p. 78.

23. Nau, *The German People*, 142.

24. The illustrations at the end of this volume are from J. Hanno Deiler, "The Settlement of the German Coast of Louisiana and the Creoles of German Descent," *Americana Germanica*, 11(1909).

Sources for Further Reading:

With regard to German-American archival holdings dealing with Louisiana'a German heritage, see "German Archives at the Historic New Orleans Collection," *The Historic New Orleans Collection: Manuscripts Division Update*, 3:1(1984): 2-7.

References to works dealing with Louisiana's German heritage can be found in Don Heinrich Tolzmann, *German-Americana: A Bibliography*, (Metuchen, N.J.: Scarecrow Pr., 1975), as well as in the same author's *Catalog of the German-Americana Collection, University of Cincinnati*, (München: K.G. Saur, 1990).

A basic starting point for anyone interested in the German heritage of Louisiana would be with the works of J. Hanno Deiler. Perhaps his best known work is his *The Settlement of the German Coast of Louisiana and the Creoles of German Descent*, (Philadelphia: Americana Germanica Pr., 1909), which appeared as a new edition edited by Jack Belsom in 1969. Marie Stella Condon has edited Deiler's *A History of the German Churches in Louisiana: 1823-1893*, (Lafayette, Louisiana: Center for Louisiana Studies, University of Southwestern Louisiana, 1983). Other works by Deiler can be found in the aforementioned bibliographcial guides. The papers of Prof. Deiler are to be found in the Historic New Orleans Collection in New Orleans, including his manuscript "Annals of the Germans of New Orleans." A copy of the Deiler Papers at the Loyaly University Library is also on file at the Historic New Orleans Collection.

The works of Karl J.R. Arndt can be found listed in Gerhard K. Friesen and Walter Schatzberg, eds., *The German Contribution to the Building of the Americas: Studies In Honor of Karl J.R. Arndt*, (Hanover, New Hampshire: Clark University Pr., 1977). A list of the

German-American newspaper and journals published in Louisiana can be found in Arndt's *German-American Newspapers and Periodicals, 1732-1955. History and Bibliography*, (Heidelberg: Quelle & Meyer, 1961), and articles dealing with the German-American press of Louisiana can be found in his *The German Language Press of the Americas: Volume 3: German-American Press Research from the American Revolution to the Bicentennial*, (München: K.G. Saur, 1980).

For the history of the colonial era of Louisiana's German heritage, there are two recent works available. Ellen C. Merrill has edited Helmut Blume, *The German Coast During the Colonial Era 1722-1803: The Evolution of a Distinct Cultural Landscape in the Lower Mississippi River Delta during the Colonial Era*, (Destrehan, Louisiana: The German-Acadian Historical and Genealogical Society, 1990). Also, dealing with the 18th century is Reinhart Kondert, *The Germans of Colonial Louisiana 1720-1803*, (Stuttgart: Akademischer Verlag, 1990).

For the first half of the 19th century, see Gustav Körner, *Das deutsche Element in den Vereinigten Staaten von Nordamerika, 1818-1848*, (Cincinnati: A.E. Wilde & Co., 1880), pp. 369-80. For the latter half of the 19th century, see John Frederick Nau, *The German People of New Orleans, 1850-1900*, (Leiden: E.J. Brill, 1958).

Of course, the present work covers the early part of the 20th century, and the "Editor's Introduction" aims to briefly bring the reader up-to-date.

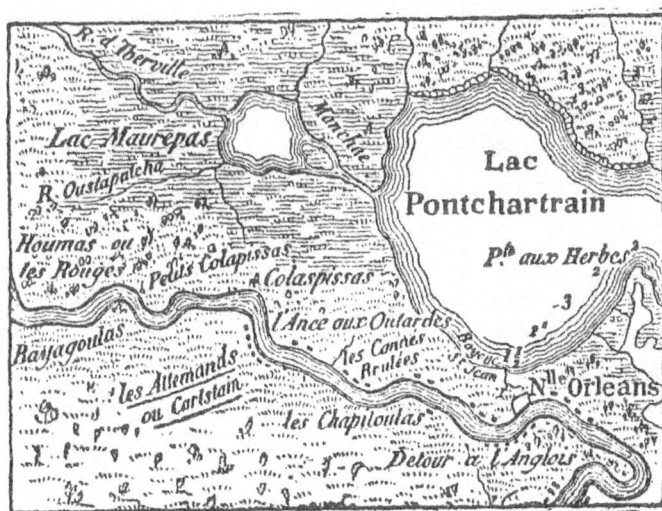

THE FIRST VILLAGES ON THE GERMAN COAST.

THE PRINCIPAL FORTS AND TRADING POSTS OF
LOUISIANA.
18TH. CENTURY.
BY
J. HANNO DEILER.

Arkansas R.

John Law's Concessions

Arkansas Post 1685

Yazoo R.

Mississippi River

Yazoo Post (Vicksburg) 1720

Black Warrior R.

Fort Toulouse 1714 +

Fort Tombeche + 1735

(Montgomery)

(Meridian)

Fort Rosalie (Natchez) 1716

Alabama R.

Tombigbee R.

Red River

Pearl R.

Bogue Chitto

Amite R.

Tuscagoula

Escambia R.

Perdido R.

Fort Louis 1702-1711

Baton Rouge 1720

Bayou Manchac

Comitee

L. Pontchartrain

Mobile + 1711
+ Krabs
o Pascagoula

1698 Pensacola

Bay of Mobile

1718 New Biloxi +

1699 + Fort Maurepas (Ocean Springs)

Deer I.

Cat I.

New Orleans 1718

L. Salvador

English Turn

Ship I. Horn I.

Dauphine I.

Pelican I.

L. Des Allemands

Des Allemands

John Law's Concession.

Bayou Lafourche

Bienvilles Fort 1699

Chandelier I.

Iberville, March 2nd. 1699

La Salle April 9th. 1682

Mississippi Delta.

Gulf   of   Mexico

Outbreak and Massacre by the Dakota Indians in Minnesota in 1862: Marion P. Satterlee's Minute Account of the Outbreak, with Exact Locations, Names of All Victims, Prisoners at Camp Release, Refugees at Fort Ridgely, etc. Complete List of Indians Killed in Battle and Those Hung, and Those Pardoned at Rock Island, Iowa

The German Element in Virginia: Herrmann Schuricht's History

The German Immigrant in America

The Pennsylvania Germans: James Owen Knauss, Jr.'s Social History

The Pennsylvania Germans: Jesse Leonard Rosenberger's Sketch of Their History and Life